D1220842

The Military Life of

GENGHIS,

Khan of Khans

THE "MILITARY LIVES" BY TREVOR N. DUPUY, COL., U.S. Army (Ret.)

The Military Life of

GENGHIS,

KHAN OF KHANS

BY TREVOR NEVITT DUPUY
Col., U.S. Army, Ret.

FRANKLIN WATTS, INC.
575 Lexington Avenue
New York, N. Y. 10022

This book is dedicated to my father,
R. Ernest Dupuy

Maps by Dyno Lowenstein

SBN 531-01877-6

Contents

Foreword

Nearly three-quarters of a century ago one of America's great military historians—Theodore Ayrault Dodge—undertook the ambitious task of writing a series of books about "the Great Captains" of history. The result was monumental: one brief summary volume on the six military leaders that Dodge considered to be "the Great Captains," and five multivolume biographies of Alexander the Great, Hannibal, Julius Caesar, Gustavus Adolphus, and Napoleon. Dodge died before he could complete his final planned work on Frederick the Great.

It does not detract from what Dodge accomplished to assert that he made one tremendous mistake in his selection of "the Great Captains." He omitted Genghis Khan.

Like so many other Westerners, Dodge dismissed Genghis Khan from consideration as simply one of a number of meteor-like Central Asian conquerors like Attila and Tamerlane, whose fleeting appearance on the stage of history was largely the result of other, more important, historical tides, and who had little if any permanent or positive effect on the subsequent course of world affairs.

In fact, however, for reasons which I hope are made abundantly clear in the following pages, Genghis Khan was not only one of the three greatest military geniuses of history, but he probably had a more significant influence on world history, even in Europe, than any other mortal man, with the possible exception of Alexander the Great.

This evaluation of Genghis Khan, which began to dawn on me when I was working with my father on a book called *Military Heritage of America*, more than fifteen years ago, has been confirmed without question in my mind by more recent research in the process of preparing an *Encyclopedia of Military History*. Genghis Khan is not only worthy of comparison with all of Dodge's "Great Captains"; as a historical figure as well as a military man, he takes precedence over most of the other six.

Unfortunately there are not many reliable works on Genghis Khan in English. This is partly because of the fact that what there is recorded about him in other languages—Chinese, Russian, French, and German—is incomplete, inconsistent, and contradictory. It is also partly due to the fact that there has apparently never before been a serious attempt at an authoritative military analysis of Genghis Khan. Hopefully the effort represented by this volume will also encourage others to try.

Because of the inadequacies, contradictions, and inconsistencies in the sources, it has sometimes been necessary to interpret what Genghis did, or why he did it, from the results rather than from the unsatisfactory reports of the events. I

x

have not hesitated to assume that a strategical and organizing genius like Genghis Khan would use sound military logic and procedures under some circumstances in which the chroniclers suggest that his actions were prompted by mysticism, or unlikely prejudice, or whim. Thus, in a few important instances in which the major sources do not make good sense, I have tried to show what *must* have happened—using some such qualifying term as "apparently"—even though there can be no proof that this was exactly the way it did occur.

In the course of preparing this book I have found that the English-language text with the most internal consistency is M. Charol's *The Mongol Empire* (first written, under the pseudonym of Michael Prawdin, in German by a Russian). Also useful is another translated book, René Grossuet's *Conqueror of the World, the Life of Chingis-Khan*, originally in French. Another important book, and probably its author's best and most scholarly, is Harold Lamb's *Genghis Khan, Emperor of All Men*. Also useful is Arthur Waley (ed.), *The Secret History of the Mongols*.

Like Grossuet, most modern scholars specializing in Chinese and Central Asian history prefer to refer to this gigantic Asian conqueror as Chingis or Jenghiz Khan. I have chosen to use the less authoritative, but better known, rendering of Genghis Khan simply because it *is* better known and generally accepted in English-language histories. Otherwise, for the most part, I have followed the Prawdin or Charol transliteration in the spelling of names and places.

I have been greatly assisted in the preparation of this book by Elizabeth Wertz—an admirer of Genghis Khan who doubts that I have done justice to him, but who hopes that my efforts may stimulate another author, who shares her views, to do a more definitive and more eulogistic biography.

T. N. DUPUY

Introduction

Temuchin began his career as a starving youth in exile. He became Genghis, Khakan (supreme ruler) of a united Mongolian nation and of the largest empire ever established by one man. He was the leader, as well as the creator, of the best army in the world during the Middle Ages.

Only an unusual person and a very gifted leader could have performed such amazing feats. From all accounts, Genghis combined intellectual brilliance, wisdom, and stability. His imaginative intelligence enabled him to plan effective strategies, and then to out-general each opponent tactically.* He planned thoroughly for each campaign and then never turned from an objective until it was achieved. The basic shrewdness, cunning, resourcefulness, and leadership qualities of Genghis Khan are evident time and again in accounts of his campaigns. When he was in an untenable military position, which did not often happen, he would still succeed and gain his ends by diplomacy or ruse.

* See Appendix for definitions of strategy and tactics, and for a discussion of the attributes of military leadership.

Yet despite his guile in warfare and diplomacy, Genghis Khan was trusted completely by his friends and allies, and with good reason. Once he assumed an alliance or a personal friendship he continued it regardless of consequences. His allies, his soldiers, and his friends could always count on his word and sturdy support. Loyalty was the quality which he valued most in other men, and he gave it in full measure himself. He never abandoned any of his warriors in battle; everyone who helped him was remembered and rewarded handsomely, just as everyone who crossed him or was disloyal or defiant was also repaid in kind.

Among his own people Genghis was universally trusted. Furthermore, he could arouse the loyalties of all people, wherever he found them—within his own tribes, among his enemies, from defeated people—and he always sought to discover men of boldness or ability. Jebei, one of his most courageous and brilliant generals, was once an enemy who shot Genghis in the neck in battle. His prime minister and confidant, Yeliu-Chutsai, was a prisoner seized from the service of the Chin emperors when Peking was captured.

Perhaps the principal characteristic of Genghis was an unsurpassed genius for organization, administration, and planning. It was this genius which created an entirely new military system and method of war, which constantly improved the techniques of warfare, and which created a stable empire. He did not like administrative details, but he devoted as much attention to these as was necessary, until he could find and develop subordinates to take over the drudgery of detail.

One vitally important demonstration of this tremendous organizing ability was the way in which Genghis delegated responsibility to trusted subordinates, and the manner in which he prepared these subordinates to accept and then to exercise this responsibility. With the possible exception of Alexander the Great, no other great general in history made such a conscious effort as Genghis to teach his lieutenants all he knew about warfare, and then to give them an opportunity to develop their talents as independent army commanders. As a result, his four sons, many of his grandsons, and at least three of his trusted *orlok* (generals) were gifted and great generals in their own rights. This is why the Mongolian Empire continued to expand under the successors of Genghis Khan for more than half a century after his death.

We do not really know what motivated this man to become the greatest conqueror in history. There is no record of what he himself may have said on the matter. He probably could not even read or write; certainly he wrote no memoirs. But from the records that are available, it does not seem that he had an insatiable appetite for conquest. By A.D. 1218 he seems to have been completely satisfied with an empire that stretched from the Great Wall to Lake Balkhash. He was a realist, however, and he wanted secure frontiers. When a neighboring country was weak and unstable, he would conquer it or annex it in order to prevent the creation of a dangerous power vacuum. But his greatest conquests—in China and Persia between 1218 and 1227—seem to have been prompted solely to avenge insults or broken treaties.

There is the possibility, on the other hand, that vengeance was merely a pretext for these great campaigns of conquest, and that he sought opportunities to establish his power and authority over all neighbors who exhibited the slightest weakness. If so, this was consistent with the cruel law of the Gobi which had previously governed the troubled relationships among the Mongol tribes; a law which Genghis learned by bitter experience as a boy and young man. But the preponderance of evidence suggests that Genghis had outgrown any such childish or primitive urge to conquer merely for the sake of conquest.

Genghis was above corruption and too well-balanced emotionally and intellectually to indulge in excesses. He adhered to the hardy, simple Mongol ways to the end of his life. He cared little for the luxuries which his vast domains provided. He was repelled by the elaborate refinements of the Chinese and Persian courts, which would later doom his descendants in those countries. He traveled with his armies, trained his sons to fight, and personally took the field as long as he was able, sharing the life of his soldiers.

That Genghis cared so little for civilization and culture accounts for all of the towns laid waste, the wide destruction in Khorassan, and the horrible atrocities for which he is remembered in Persian literature. But it also accounts for the endurance and strength with which he waged his campaigns, suffered many hardships, and displayed his grim determination. He never wavered in a project he had begun; he simply kept on fighting, scheming, and planning until the task was done.

Genghis gave his mother credit for making him what he

was. He claimed that she took him and his brothers and "raised them up by the shoulders to be men." As to personal habits, Genghis, like all Mongols, enjoyed fermented liquor. He drank and celebrated along with his companions. Also, like all Mongols who could afford the expense, he had several wives. But Bortei, his first wife, was always honored. His sons by his several marriages all loved him, respected him, and worked with him on all his undertakings.

A terror to his foes, responsible for more death and destruction than perhaps any other man, Genghis was, nevertheless, a good, wise, and respectable man when judged according to the customs of his time and people. And he was one of the three greatest generals the world has ever known.

The Military Life of

GENGHIS,
Khan of Khans

CHAPTER 1

The Fugitive

A Prince in Exile

In the year 1162 Yesukai the Strong, chief of the Kiut subclan of the Borjigin Mongols, was presented with his eldest son. The boy was named Temuchin and was brought up to be a fighter and hunter, as befitted a future chieftain. Temuchin was only thirteen when Yesukai was treacherously killed by Tartar poison.

The Kiuts, a tribe of some 40,000 tents or families, were nomads who lived in the steppes and mountains north of the Gobi Desert. The ancestral grazing grounds of the tribe were in the valleys where the headwaters of the Tula, Onon, and Kemlen rivers rise—about 150 miles northeast of modern Ulan Bator.

The Kiuts moved from place to place in this region, hunting their food and herding their cattle. Life was precarious in that desolate region of Central Asia. Each Mongol tribe was alert for any sign of weakness among its neighbors, hoping for an opportunity to destroy a weaker tribe. This was a cruel, harsh process. All the men would be killed; the women and

1

children would be enslaved; the cattle and everything else of value would be seized.

The Kiut tribe was fearful that this might be their fate without a strong leader, and they did not believe that a boy of thirteen could provide strong leadership. Although Temuchin was now the lawful ruler, the people turned for leadership to Targutai, the cousin of Yesukai, and leader of the neighboring Taijiut subclan.

Temuchin's mother, Yulun-Eke, tried in vain to rally some of the people to support her son. But the Kiuts voted to accept Targutai as leader and stripped Temuchin's family of all their possessions and drove them out into the desert. Everybody expected that the outcasts would soon die of starvation in the rugged climate.

For several months Temuchin, with his mother, three brothers, two half-brothers, and a sister, had a desperate struggle for survival. They ate any food they could find—berries, onions, garlic, fish, and small animals. They hid in the foothills of Mount Burkan-Kaldun (now called Kentei, or Hentey), to prevent the tribe from learning that they were still alive. Temuchin and Kasar, his brother, killed one of their half-brothers, Bektor, for eating more than his share of food. The other half-brother, Belgutei, remained Temuchin's loyal supporter.

Eventually Targutai heard that Temuchin was alive and decided to kill him so that the boy would not grow up to dispute his rule. Targutai and his Taijiut and Kiut warriors searched through the hills until they found Temuchin's ragged camp.

Temuchin and his family had fled, but Targutai's men caught up with Temuchin and captured him. They put his head in a kang (a wooden collar which also held the arms out straight), then celebrated their success before killing him. But while the other Mongols were drinking great quantities of fermented mare's milk, Sorgan-Shira, a warrior friendly to Temuchin's father, set him free. The boy escaped from the drunken Mongols; he soon found his family, and they went back into hiding in the wooded hills.

The story of Temuchin's escape soon spread among his Kiut clansmen, who began to talk admiringly of his success. This annoyed Targutai, who again sent his warriors to find Temuchin. But though Targutai kept trying, never again did he or his men find Temuchin. Targutai became upset by these failures because the people began to realize they had made a mistake when they had made him chief of the tribe instead of Temuchin. Soon deserters from the Kiut tribe began to join Temuchin in his hiding place.

The first of these deserters was a lad named Bogurchi, about Temuchin's age. Jelmi, son of an old friend of Yesukai, was his second vassal. More and more young warriors came to cast their lot with Temuchin. With his followers he went to the chief of a nearby small tribe to claim his daughter, Bortei, as his bride. The clever young Temuchin was now seventeen, with gray eyes "that did not slant," long reddish-brown braids, and skin well seasoned in the wind and sun. Bortei thought that the outlaw prince was attractive, and was happy to marry him. From her father Temuchin gained more followers.

3

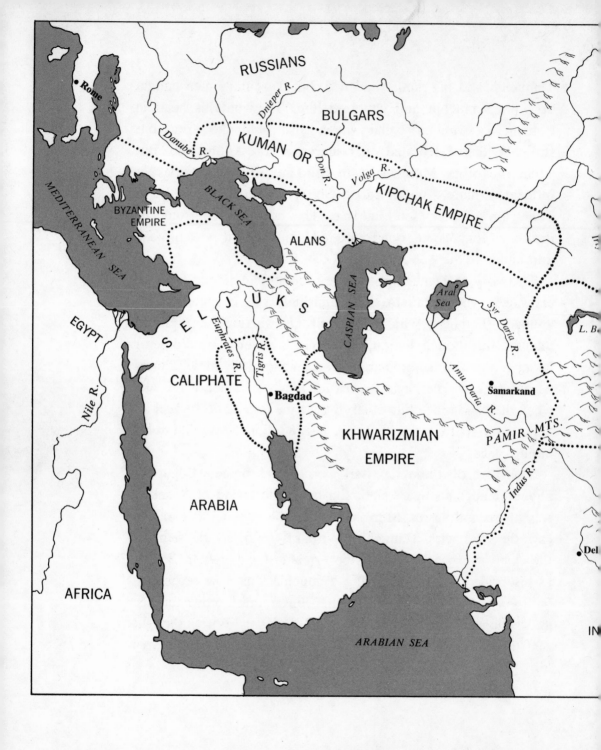

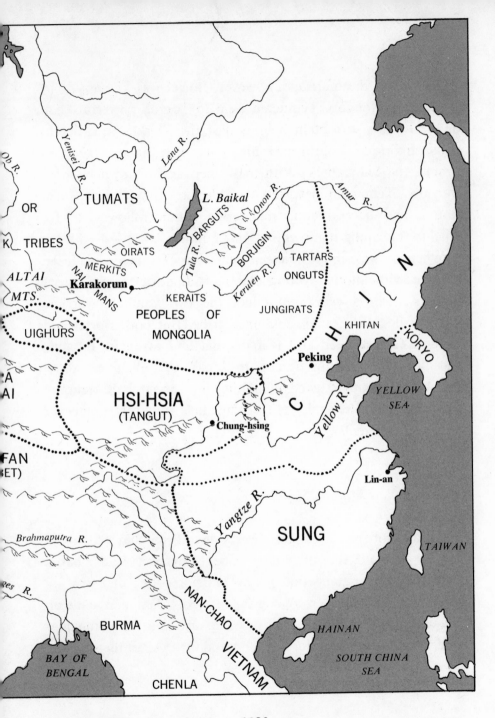

People and Kingdoms of Asia, c. 1180 A.D.

Soon after the marriage, however, Bortei was kidnapped by the Merkit Mongols. Temuchin went to Togrul, powerful khan of the Keraits, to obtain help against the Merkits in order to regain his bride. Togrul gave him some men for an expedition against the kidnappers. With these men and his own band of warriors, Temuchin devasted the Merkit camp and regained Bortei. The success of this raid brought more followers to Temuchin, including many entire Kiut families.

When he was about nineteen years old, Temuchin made an alliance with another young chieftain, Jamuga, of the Juriat Mongols. For a year and a half the two youthful warriors jointly ruled their small combined tribe. But both Bortei and Yulun-Eke distrusted and feared cruel and arrogant Jamuga, and finally Temuchin agreed to break the alliance. About half of the people stayed with him, and about half went off with Jamuga. After this split, Temuchin's followers numbered about 13,000 tents.

A New Military System

It was probably about this time, when Temuchin was about twenty years old, that the young leader adopted a regular battle formation and organization for his warriors—one that was apparently completely new among the Mongols. Ten men made up a squad, ten squads made up a company, and ten companies made a group, or *guran*, of one thousand men. All of the warriors were mounted on horses.

Temuchin started with thirteen gurans. By means of daily exercises and games he trained his warriors to ride, turn, and attack as units until they became extremely skillful in riding and fighting together. He made his men practice constantly with their longbows, and trained them to fight side by side as a team in hand-to-hand combat in the thick of battle. Because they trained and practiced as units, Temuchin's men could move without delay in response to his orders. Never before had Mongols observed such discipline. Temuchin chose the best and strongest warriors as the leaders of his gurans, and demanded that they give him immediate and absolute obedience. Each guran leader demanded and received the same obedience from his men.

Such training, organization, and discipline were important a few years later, in 1188, when Targutai attacked Temuchin. Targutai, who was fearful of Temuchin's growing strength, attacked when Temuchin was moving camp with his warriors, their families, cattle, and wagons. By this time Temuchin had perhaps 20,000 warriors, but Targutai had more than 30,000. However, Temuchin was warned by his scouts of Targutai's approach, and prepared for defense.

The usual method of defense by the Mongols was to place their wagons in a ring or laager (like the American settlers of the plains) and then all the warriors would fight from inside. Temuchin, however, decided that he would fight differently. He placed his more heavily armed units in a line in front of a thick forest, and behind a screen of his light cavalry. Each guran was drawn up in formation 100 men wide and 10 men deep. He

7

placed the wagon laager at the very end of one wing, to be defended by the women and children.

Targutai's horsemen advanced in an irregular line on a 5-mile front toward the waiting defenders. When they came within range, Temuchin's light cavalrymen fired a volley of arrows, then moved to the rear, behind Temuchin's main line of heavily armed cavalry. The solid units of heavy cavalry then charged against Targutai's men, quickly overwhelming them. The Kiut and Taijiut warriors had never before experienced the powerful shock of a massed cavalry charge, and 6,000 were killed. Targutai was one of the many prisoners, and he was executed by order of Temuchin.

The young chieftain now demanded and received the allegiance of all of the defeated warriors of the Kiut tribe. At last, after thirteen years of exile, Temuchin had become the unquestioned leader of his father's tribe. Some of the leaderless Taijiuts also acknowledged him as their chieftain.

Such astounding success was bound to attract more Mongols who wished to join such a great and powerful leader. Temuchin was recognized as one of the most powerful of the tribal leaders of the Borjigin Mongols.

CHAPTER 2

Emperor of the Mongols

Khan of the Borjigins

At the age of twenty-eight, in the year 1190, Temuchin was chosen Khan of the Borjigin Mongols by a Kuriltai, or council of the chiefs. Four of his relatives—Altan, Kuchar, Sacha-beki, and Daaritai—had claimed the title also, and none of them was happy when Temuchin was chosen. However, the title of Khan was not very important among the Borjigin at this time. All the tribal chiefs of the clan were very jealous of their prerogatives and when they elected Temuchin they had no intention of appointing a master over themselves. They simply saw their new Khan as a leader only in time of war and in great hunts, and they expected that he would leave them alone most of the time.

But Temuchin had other ideas; he had begun to see the possibility of a Mongol nation and of a permanent, well-trained army. The first thing he did after he became Khan was to create a Borjigin army, based on the system he had established for his own tribe. He appointed the best Borjigin warriors to be *orlok*, or generals. Among the first of these orlok were men who would later become great leaders under his guidance: Jelmi, Jebei, Bogurchi, Sorgan-Shira, Mukuli, Kasar, and youthful Sabutai.

Temuchin also set up a messenger service which was to keep him in constant touch with all the scattered tribes of the clan. These "arrow messengers," as they were called, wrapped themselves in bandages to protect their bodies from buffeting and shaking and fatigue during long hours in the saddle at high speed. They took great pride in their skill and endurance.

Alliance with the Keraits

About this time the Chin emperors of northern China were recruiting Mongols to fight for them against the fierce Tartar tribes of eastern Mongolia. The Chinese had traditionally kept the nomads of the border regions in check by playing them off against each other, and this was why they had called on the Mongols to fight the Tartars, who were at that time seriously threatening their frontiers.

Temuchin sent a message to his old ally, Togrul, khan of the powerful Kerait Mongols of central Mongolia, suggesting that their two clans fight jointly for the Chinese. Togrul agreed, and the Borjigins and Keraits won several great victories for the Chin Dynasty in 1194. The Chinese rewarded Temuchin and Togrul handsomely and gave them titles as "defenders of the border." The two Mongol khans continued for some time to be quite close as friends and allies, hunting together and giving each other assistance when it was requested.

Most of the other Mongol clans feared this powerful alliance. So, in 1201, the Jungirats, Merkits, Oirats, Taijiuts, Naimans, and some Tartars banded together in an opposing alliance. They selected Jamuga as their leader and named him Gur Khan, or Leader of the Peoples.

Jamuga at once collected an allied army, which he led in an attack on the Borjigins. But although they were outnumbered, Temuchin's disciplined forces easily defeated the attackers, then overran and subdued the remaining Mongol and Tartar tribes of eastern Mongolia. In some of these tribes, particularly among the Tartars, Temuchin killed all the adult males, took the women for his own clan, and adopted many of the children into his own tribe and family. As a result of these victories, Temuchin became the unchallenged leader of eastern Mongolia. Jamuga fled to seek the protection of the Naiman clan of western Mongolia.

The Broken Alliance

In central Mongolia, meanwhile, Togrul's friendship with Temuchin was being undermined by the Kerait khan's son, Sengun, who feared and envied Temuchin. Sengun, suspecting that Temuchin might try to succeed his father as leader of the Kerait clan, formed an alliance with Jamuga against Temuchin. The two plotters persuaded the aging Togrul to approve their

11

plans. Reluctantly, Togrul assembled a combined Kerait-Naiman army in preparation for an invasion of Borjigin lands. Learning of this, Temuchin hastily gathered part of his army and marched west into Kerait territory to forestall the invasion.

We do not know the size of the opposing armies, but Temuchin was greatly outnumbered. Also his enemies had begun to copy his organization and methods of warfare. The two armies met in central Mongolia and fought a bloody, inconclusive battle. Temuchin, realizing that he would need more men, withdrew eastward, sending messengers to call up the warriors of all of the tribes of eastern Mongolia.

The chieftains of the eastern Mongols resented Temuchin's call to arms. They felt he had no right to issue such an order without a kuriltai, and most of them refused him aid. Temuchin therefore had to retreat to eastern Mongolia, closely pursued by the Keraits and Naimans. It was a bitter, grueling march, with many hard-fought rearguard actions. Usually Mongol warriors would desert a defeated general, but in this crisis most of Temuchin's men remained loyal. When the march was over he appointed all of those who had retreated with him members of the Order of Ter Khans. These were the men who ever afterward were always closest to Temuchin and to whom he gave great wealth and honors. They were allowed nine capital offenses without punishment. They were given complete freedom to enter his tent at any time.

After he reached his own lands, Temuchin was able to persuade most of his chieftains to support him. And as his army grew, Togrul, Sengun, and Jamuga ceased their pursuit and returned to central Mongolia.

In the months that followed, the alliance between the Keraits and the Naimans fell apart. At the same time there was increasing unrest among the Keraits, many of whom admired Temuchin and were becoming resentful of Togrul's authority. One Kerait chieftain, Daaritai, deserted to Temuchin and brought him word of the squabbles among his enemies.

Kasar, one of Temuchin's brothers, had been captured by Togrul, but he escaped and rejoined Temuchin. At Temuchin's suggestion Kasar sent a message to Togrul, saying that Temuchin was dead and that he, Kasar, wished to accept Togrul's leadership again. When Togrul received this message, he prepared a feast to welcome Kasar and to celebrate Temuchin's death.

Temuchin and his army were meanwhile marching at full speed into central Mongolia. They caught the Keraits by surprise in the middle of their celebration and defeated them completely. Togrul and Sengun escaped from the disaster and fled west, but were both killed later by the Naimans when they sought sanctuary. The cruel Naiman king, Baibuka Tayan, had Togrul's head mounted on his throne. Meanwhile, most of the Kerait warriors joined Temuchin's army.

Struggle for Mongolia

Temuchin now ruled central and eastern Mongolia and he consolidated these regions into one empire. Of all the Mongol peoples, only the Naimans of western Mongolia did not acknowledge him as their khan. The Naimans were a com-

13

paratively civilized people; they had a written language and looked down on the other Mongols as illiterate barbarians.

Baibuka Tayan decided to fight Temuchin before Temuchin became any stronger. But Temuchin had established a network of spies in the Naiman country, and he found out about Baibuka Tayan's plans through his intelligence service. Early in 1204 Temuchin called a kuriltai, informed his chieftains of the Naiman plans, and asked them to support him in an invasion of the Naiman country. With the help of the orlok, the Ter Khans, and his brothers, Temuchin succeeded in persuading a majority of his chieftains to vote for war. He then headed west for the Naiman territory, with an army that was probably about 80,000 strong.

Baibuka Tayan had a force of equal size, made up of Naimans, Merkits, and some Tartars. Jamuga was his second-in-command. The Naiman army assembled near the junction of the Selenga and Orkhon rivers, north of Karakorum, the Naiman capital, at a place called Chakirmont, to await Temuchin's advance.

When Temuchin's scouts sighted the Naimans, he halted his army and prepared for battle. While Temuchin's troops were deploying in combat formation, they were suddenly attacked. The overeager Naiman generals had charged without orders, but their attack was not coordinated. Temuchin's disciplined troops repulsed the Naimans and then overran them. By his victory in this Battle of Chakirmont, Temuchin became master of all of Mongolia.

Temuchin now was generous to the defeated Naimans. There

14

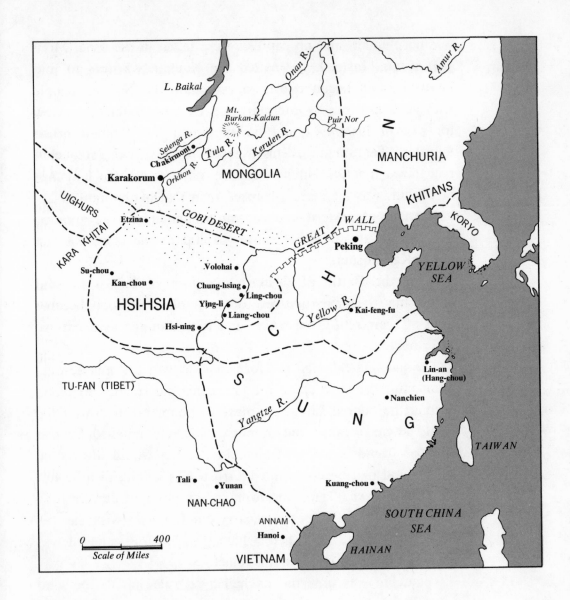

Mongolia and the Kingdoms of China, c. 1205

was no plunder, and no captives were taken in the usual Mongol custom. Instead, he invited the Naiman warriors to join his army, and began efforts to assimilate the Naiman people with his own tribes by intermarriage. He took Baibuka's widow for one of his wives and he appointed the Naiman prime minister, Tatatungo, as his Keeper of the Seal. Temuchin recognized that the Naiman culture, with its written language of Uighur, was far more advanced than that of the more primitive tribes of eastern and central Mongolia. So, he adopted this culture and moved his own capital to the chief Naiman city of Karakorum.

After the Battle of Chakirmont, Jamuga and a handful of his men became fugitives. But his followers soon became tired of their pitiful existence, and took Jamuga as a captive to Temuchin.

The meeting between the former allies was a dramatic one. Temuchin wished to spare the life of his old friend and blood brother; he offered Jamuga a place of honor in his army if he would swear loyalty. But Jamuga, sincerely touched by this offer of friendship, told Temuchin that he would always be jealous and that he could not be trusted as a faithful follower. He proudly asked Temuchin to have him put to death. Sorrowfully Temuchin gave orders to carry out Jamuga's wish; he was strangled without bloodshed, which the Mongols believed was the honorable kind of death for a chief.

Temuchin was now the unchallenged ruler of all the land from Siberia to China, with 400,000 tents and a population of more than 2,000,000 people. In 1206 a kuriltai of all the

16

Mongol chiefs assembled at Karakorum and appointed Temuchin as their Khakan (Khan of Khans). They also gave
him the title of Genghis, a new word in the Mongol language.
Some think it came from the Turkic word for "ocean," mean-
ing that his dominion spread out over all the earth. Others believe it was a completely new word, resembling the Mongol
terms for "great," "unflinching," and "invincible."

For the first time one ruler was able to command the
loyalty and respect of previously lawless and warlike bands of
Mongol nomads. Genghis Khan (as we shall now call him)
instilled in these people a feeling of pride in themselves as Mongols. He taught his people to think of themselves as an important and honorable nation, rather than as a loose con-
federation of tribes.

That these highly independent people could so quickly be
formed into one nation may seen incredible. Yet after 1206 their
internal rivalries ceased and they gave their full loyalty to
their newly created Mongol nation and its leader. They entered
his armies and obeyed his laws and orders from then on without question. This abrupt change was due entirely to the
strength and prestige of the new Khakan.

Soon after he established his empire, Genghis Khan originated
his famous Yasak, or Code of Laws. He named his adopted
brother, a Tartar prince named Shigi Kutuku, Grand Judge
to administer the laws. Like most of Genghis' appointments,
this was successful and the Grand Judge displayed a real
talent for settling disputes.

Genghis' heart was in the organization and training of his

17

army. He appointed a Commander of the West, Bogurchi, and a Commander of the East, Mukuli. An expanded arrow messenger service was established under Jelmi. The Khan's personal bodyguard of 1,000 men was commanded by Jebei Noyon. Genghis kept a contingent of 10,000 warriors under arms in and around his capital or headquarters at all times as a kind of standing army. Since these men were all sons of chiefs, he converted the landed aristocracy into his personal army, accounting in part for the total lack of opposition among the Mongols to his leadership.

Mongol Military Organization

Genghis now energetically devoted his efforts to establishing his military organization throughout all of Mongolia, and in training and equipping all Mongol warriors to fight in accordance with his now well-established methods of warfare. Although he kept only a standing force of about 11,000 men under arms in times of peace, he frequently called up large tribal contingents for training, or for maneuvers, or for great hunts—which were really a disguised form of war games.

Genghis retained his decimal system of organization, with squads of 10 men, squadrons of 100, and regiments, or gurans, of 1,000 men. Ten of these gurans were combined into a *touman*, or division, of 10,000 horsemen. Two or three, or sometimes more, *toumans* were combined into a horde, or army corps.

The hunt

Every Mongol soldier was a horseman. All were expert in the use of weapons; they had been riders from early youth, brought up in the harsh school of the Gobi Desert. They were accustomed to hardships and all extremes of weather. These simple men were not interested in luxuries or rich food; they had strong bodies and needed little or no medical attention to keep fit for operations.

The commander of each Mongol unit was selected on the basis of individual ability and valor on the field of battle. He exercised absolute authority over his unit, subject to equally strict control and supervision from his superior. All officers knew that they would be demoted for failure to perform their duties well and that good performance would be rewarded with promotion. Instant obedience to orders was demanded and received; not since the time of the Romans had discipline been so strictly enforced. Looting in battle or in a captured city was forbidden until the operation was completed and the enemy subdued. Yet mutual trust and loyalty existed between all ranks, from highest to lowest.

About two-thirds of the soldiers were light cavalrymen; the remainder were equipped with heavier armor and weapons. The light horsemen were almost all armed with the long Mongol bow and a quiver of arrows. In addition they usually carried either a lasso, or a sheaf of javelins, and wore a light sword or battle-ax slung from the belt or from the horse's saddle. For protection they carried a leather-covered wicker shield and usually wore a helmet and sometimes a leather jerkin, but never wore full body armor.

The heavy cavalrymen rode sturdier horses than the more lightly armed warriors. They also carried shields, and wore complete leather body armor, sometimes covered with scales or rings of iron or steel. The principal heavy-cavalry weapon was the lance, and every heavy horseman was also armed with a large scimitar or battle-ax. Many of them also carried a bow and a quiver of arrows slung across their backs.

When going into battle all soldiers—light and heavy—wore a shirt of heavy, raw silk next to their skin. Genghis had discovered that an arrow would rarely penetrate the silk. And so, when a soldier was wounded with an arrow, his comrades could easily withdraw it from the flesh by gently pulling on

Mongolian archers

the silk cloth. Because of this, and because wounded soldiers sucked each other's wounds, there was much less loss of life from infection than in other armies of the Middle Ages. It was a matter of principle and of honor that no wounded soldiers would be abandoned in battle and that aid would be given to every stricken man whenever the course of battle would permit it.

Every soldier had two or three horses. During a march the extra mounts would be herded along behind a touman. When speed was required, the troops would change their horses two or three times a day, to keep the horses from getting too tired. If possible, the troops always changed to fresh horses before a battle. This system of extra mounts was one of the reasons why the Mongols could march for days at a time at rates of speed that were incredible to their enemies.

Mongolian horsemen

Usually the Mongol horseman's mounts were mares. When either food or water was scarce, particularly in long marches across the steppes, the soldiers could refresh themselves, or keep themselves alive by drinking mare's milk. And even on the desolate steppes the horses could usually find enough grass for grazing.

Their almost complete reliance upon their horses sometimes created military problems for the armies of Genghis Khan. When grass or other fodder was poor or scarce, the Mongols had to keep moving, so that they could find fresh grazing land. This was one reason why Genghis preferred to campaign in winter; his tough, sturdy horses could usually find green grass beneath the snow on land that would be completely dry and dusty in summertime. Another reason for winter campaigns was so that his cavalry armies could move swiftly across ice-

bound rivers and frozen swamps which would be serious ob- —
stacles in warmer weather.

Mongol Training, Tactics, and Strategy*

We know little of the details of the training system of Genghis
Khan. We do know that each troop, squadron, and regiment
was capable of precise performance of battle-drill movements
that formed the basis of Mongol small-unit tactics. Such precision required constant practice under close and demanding
supervision. The amazingly successful battlefield coordination
of units within the toumans, and among toumans and the
larger hordes, is evidence that Genghis insisted on painstaking
drill-field practice by forces of all sizes.

The mobility of Genghis Khan's troops has never been
matched by other ground soldiery. No other commander in
history has been more aware of the importance of seizing
and maintaining the initiative. His troops always attacked,
even when their strategic mission was defensive.

At the outset of a campaign, the Mongol toumans usually
advanced rapidly on an extremely broad front, maintaining
only messenger contact between major elements. When an
enemy force was found, it became the objective of all nearby
Mongol units. Complete information regarding enemy location,
strength, and direction of movement was immediately sent by
messenger to central headquarters, and in turn this information

* See Appendix for a discussion of tactics and strategy.

23

Mongol camp

was passed on to all field units. If the enemy force was small, it was dealt with promptly by the local commanders. If it was too large to be disposed of so readily, the main Mongol army would rapidly concentrate behind an active cavalry screen. Frequently a rapid advance would overwhelm separate sections of an enemy army before its concentration could be completed.

Genghis and his capable subordinates avoided repeated patterns in their advances to combat. If the enemy's location were definitely determined, they might lead the bulk of their forces to strike him in the rear, or to turn his flank. Often they would pretend to retreat, only to return at the charge on fresh horses.

24

Most frequent

Most frequently, however, the Mongols would advance to battle behind a screen of light horsemen in several roughly parallel columns, spread across a wide front. This permitted flexibility, particularly if the enemy were strong or if his exact location was not firmly determined. The column encountering the main opposing force would then engage the enemy or retire if his strength were too great. Meanwhile the other columns would continue to advance, occupying the country to the enemy's flank and rear. This would usually force the opposing general to fall back, to protect his line of communications. The Mongols would then close in from all sides to take advantage of any confusion or disorder in the enemy's retirement. This was usually followed by his eventual encirclement and destruction.

The Mongol cavalry squadrons, because of their precision, their concerted action, their skilled use of weapons, and their amazing mobility, were much superior to all other troops they encountered, even when the opponents were more heavily or better armed, or more numerous. The rapidity of the Mongol movements almost always gave them superiority of force at the decisive point, which is the ultimate aim of all battle tactics. By seizing the initiative, and making the utmost use of their mobility, Genghis Khan and his subordinate commanders, rather than their foes, almost always selected the point and time of decision.

The battle formation was composed of five lines of horsemen, each of a single rank, with large intervals between each line. Heavy cavalry made up the first two lines; the other three were lighter horsemen. Reconnaissance and screening were carried out in front of these lines by other lighter cavalry units. As the op-

25

posing forces drew nearer to each other, the three rear ranks of light cavalry advanced through intervals in the two heavy lines to shower the enemy with a withering fire of well-aimed javelins and deadly arrows from their powerful longbows.

The intensive firepower preparation would usually shake even the boldest of foes. Sometimes this harassment would scatter the enemy without need for any further action. When the touman commander felt that the enemy had been sufficiently confused by the missile preparation, the light horsemen would be ordered to retire, and synchronized signals would start the heavy cavalry on its charge.

In addition to combining fire and movement—and missile action with shock action—Genghis Khan also emphasized maneuver and all kinds of tactical diversions. During a hard-fought engagement, a portion of the Mongol force usually held the enemy's attention by frontal attack. While the opposing commander was thus diverted, the remainder of the army would deliver a decisive blow on the flank or rear.

Genghis Khan's genius as an organizer and as a strategical and tactical leader has probably never been excelled, and has been matched by few other generals in history. He utilized surprise, mobility, offensive action, concentrated force, and diversionary tactics to overwhelm armies which were usually more numerous, and frequently better armed.

CHAPTER 3

War Against Hsi-Hsia—Western China (1206–1210)

The Challenge of China

The new Mongol nation had three powerful neighbors. The Chin Empire of northern China was to the southeast; the Tangut (or Tibetan kingdom), called Hsi-Hasi, lay to the south and southwest; and the Chinese-Uighur kingdom of Kara-Khitai was farther west. The Chins of northern China considered themselves the successors of the old, powerful Chinese Empire of the T'ang and Sung dynasties. They did not like the idea of a new, consolidated Mongol nation, since for ages the Chinese had fostered dissension among the divided nomad tribes of central Asia so that they would keep each other weak.

Many of these lands—even most of Mongolia—had once belonged to the Chinese Empire, before it broke up in the tenth century as a result of an invasion of Khitan Mongols from Manchuria. The Khitans adopted Chinese culture and established the Liao dynasty of northern China. They were soon overthrown by more invaders from further north in Manchuria, and Jurchens, who also soon began to adopt Chinese customs, and established the Chin dynasty. The last of the Liao princes had fled to the west with some of his followers and had formed the kingdom of Kara-Khitai in Uighur country. In south China, the old Sung dynasty still ruled. Meanwhile the Tangut people of western China had gained their independence from the Sung in the eleventh century, to establish Hsi-Hsia.

Genghis realized that he would some day have to deal with one or more of these neighbors. But he considered that the Chin of north China, the former Jurchens, were the most dangerous. So he sent his spies to gain all possible information about the country and its armies. He learned that the Chin Empire was a rich, powerful country defended by massive fortresses and walled cities. The armies were large, well trained, and well organized.

Genghis decided, therefore, to try to avoid war with the Chin until after he had dealt with Hsi-Hsia. This was modeled after the Chinese state, and had similar armies and fortresses. But the armies were not so strong or so well organized and the cities were not so strongly defended. Hsi-Hsia would make a good training ground for the inevitable struggle with the Chin of China.

Invasions of Hsi-Hsia

Genghis led his Mongol armies in invasions of Hsi-Hsia three times—in 1205, 1207, and 1209. In 1205 and 1207 the Mongols easily defeated the Hsi-Hsia cavalry in combat in the plains. But they were baffled by the fortresses and walled cities. At the Hsi-Hsia walled city of Volohai, the splendid cavalry of

Genghis was completely at a loss in the campaign of 1207. The inhabitants would not come out to fight and the Mongols could not get in. They knew nothing about besieging a fortress or walled town.

Genghis finally gained by trickery what he could not accomplish by fighting. He sent messengers saying that the siege would be raised and the Mongols would leave if the people of Volohai would pay tribute of one thousand cats and ten thousand swallows. The people thought he must be crazy, but they captured the cats and birds, and sent them in tribute just in order to get rid of the invaders. The Mongols tied wool to the tails of each animal and bird, then lighted the wool and set the animals loose. The maddened cats and birds at once tried to return home, into the city. Soon fires broke out all over town. In the resulting confusion, the Mongols were able to climb over the walls, open the gates, and capture the city.

After this success, Genghis obtained a promise of yearly tribute from Li An-ch'uan, the Hsi-Hsia emperor, then left. The Mongol troops were disappointed by the negotiated peace, because they believed that they could conquer all of Hsi-Hsia. But Genghis knew that even though his troops could defeat the Tangut armies, they needed training in the art of siegecraft before they could conquer the country. Certainly they could never attack the Chin Empire with their present state of training and equipment.

Returning to Mongolia, Genghis sent out messengers to gather all of the tribal leaders and orlok. He told them that he was establishing a new War Academy, which they would have to

29

attend. He then instituted a course in siegecraft to supplement their yearly war games and maneuvers, and the daily drills of the cavalry. All of the lessons learned at Volohai were reviewed. Each tribe was directed to prepare a siege train—complete with storming ladders, huge shields, and sandbags. When the course was finished, the leaders returned to their tribes and to their toumans to assemble the siege trains and to instruct their men in the new type of warfare.

In 1209, Genghis returned to Hsi-Hsia with a more serious expedition. To reach the country his 80,000 soldiers crossed 450 miles of the Gobi Desert. Near the border, at Wu-la-hai, they were met by an army of 50,000 men, under Hsi-Hsia Prince Li Tsun-hsiang and General Kao Liang-hui. The Mongols easily defeated this force and captured the enemy leaders. They then moved on and easily captured the rebuilt fortress of Volohai, using their new siege techniques.

Genghis then moved on toward the capital city, Chung-hsing (now Ninghsia) on the Yellow River. Just outside the city he was met by an army of 120,000 men under General Wei-ming Ling-Kung. Genghis used one of his favorite tricks by pretending to retreat. The Hsi-Hsia army followed, and were attacked from ambush by the waiting Mongols. The Hsi-Hsia army was crushed, and the commanding general was taken prisoner. The Mongols then moved on to attack the capital.

Genghis soon learned that the defenses of Chung-hsing were much more formidable than those of Volohai. He grimly settled down to a siege, and for two months the Mongols vainly attempted to fight their way in. Then Genghis devised the plan of diverting the waters of the Yellow River away from the city. But the Yellow River has never been tamed easily. The dam broke; the Mongol camps in the plains were flooded and the besiegers were forced to move to higher ground. Genghis then sent captured Tanguts into the city as messengers, to demand tribute. The emperor was assured that if the tribute were paid, the Mongols would leave the country.

Li An-ch'uan paid the tribute, since the invasion was disrupting the trade of his country. The Silk Road from China to Persia passed through Hsi-Hsia and the economy of the country depended on this trade. He gave Genghis some rare white camels, woolen cloth, falcons, and the promise of military assistance in the future. He also gave his daughter to Genghis as a wife, showing his recognition of the overlordship of Genghis. Thus in the year 1210 the Mongols completed the Hsi-Hsia expedition and returned in triumph to Mongolia.

The Chin Empire

In the meantime, the elderly Chin emperor had died. The new Emperor Wei-wang sent an embassy to Genghis demanding his homage. Genghis refused to acknowledge the new emperor as his overlord, spitting contemptuously when he was told the news. When this was reported to Emperor Wei-wang he threw the ambassadors into prison as punishment for bringing bad news. He made plans to send an army to punish this upstart Mongol chieftain who had once been his father's vassal. Although no action was taken to carry out these plans, Genghis decided that this was a cause for war, and made plans himself for an invasion of the Chin Empire.

While Genghis was collecting and readying his armies in Mongolia, during the late months of 1210, he welcomed his eldest son, Juji, who returned with the two orlok Jebei and Sabutai from a campaign beyond the western borders of Mongolia. The reasons for this campaign are obscure, but apparently Genghis had been concerned about the activities of the fugitive Naiman and Merkit chieftains among the Turkish Kirghiz, or Kipchak, tribes, in the vast region north of Lake Balkhash. After the defeat at Chakrimont, it seems that Guchluk, son of Baibuka, the Naiman khan who had been killed in the battle, and Toto, khan of the Merkits, had fled into this region with a number of their warriors. By 1208 they had obtained sufficient power and influence among the Kipchak to become a threat to Genghis' empire again.

Apparently Genghis considered leading the expedition into the Kipchak region himself, and some historians believe that he, and not Juji, was in command. It does not seem likely, however, that Genghis would have believed that this threat was great enough to require him to abandon his efforts against the Hsi-Hsia. He was certainly campaigning in Hsi-Hsia in 1209 and 1210, and the records indicate that the expedition into the Kipchak region did not return to central Mongolia until 1210.

Either late in 1208 or early in 1209 Juji and his force met and defeated a Mongol-Kipchak army under Guchluk and Toto, on the banks of the Irtysh River. Toto was killed;

Guchluk and a few survivors fled southwestward into the land of the Kara-Khitai. Following his victory, Juji subdued the Kipchak tribes. He then returned to Karakorum, bringing with him the chiefs of some of these mountain tribes, who promised to provide men for the forthcoming operations in China. Genghis was so pleased with Juji's conduct of this expedition that he gave him all of the lands of the west "as far as a Mongol pony can travel" to be his inheritance.

Genghis had also sent Belgutei, his half-brother, into the Yenisei River region of Siberia, to subdue the Tumats and bring them under Mongol rule. But Belgutei was killed in battle, and his troops failed to conquer the Tumats. Genghis resolved that he would deal with the Tumats after his return from China. He would also punish Kara-Khitai in the southwest, which was harboring the fugitive son of Baibuka Tayan, the former chief of the Naimans. But now he realized he must put these plans aside and concentrate upon the foe beyond the eastern borders—the Chin of north China.

The Mongol armies, along with all the allies Genghis could muster, assembled in a great camp area on the Kerulen River during the winter of 1210–11. In February the vast host, probably about 200,000 men, began to march slowly southeastward across the Gobi Desert toward the Great Wall of China.

CHAPTER 4

The Conquest of North China
(1211–1215)

First Campaign Against the Chin (1211)

By early spring of 1211 the scouts of the Mongol army had reached the Great Wall. In accordance with his usual custom, many months earlier Genghis had sent spies ahead to learn all that they could about the Chinese armies, the fortifications of their cities, and their plans for defense. From the information received from these spies, Genghis realized that he was facing a truly formidable enemy. He recognized that failure to win a decisive victory might be as serious as a defeat. If he did not win his followers would be likely to desert him, in typical Mongol fashion, ending the existence of his newly established Mongol nation.

Genghis left only 20,000 warriors to guard Mongolia. All other able-bodied men had been called up to join the invasion of the Chin Empire. The three eldest of Genghis' sons—Juji, Jagatai, and Ogatai—each commanded a horde of about four toumans. Genghis commanded a similar force, keeping

34

with him his youngest son, Tuli, to teach him more about the art of war. A fifth horde was commanded by Jebei.

The five hordes advanced toward the Great Wall on a broad front. Genghis was kept informed of the progress of the other four hordes by his usual excellent messenger service. Genghis insisted that his generals report exactly what they found, informing him of bad news as well as good.

Meanwhile the Chin emperor in Peking* had learned nothing about the advancing Mongol host. The outlying Chinese officials knew that messengers bringing bad news to the emperor were often imprisoned, and the originator punished. This meant that the emperor could not expect to receive accurate information.

The Ongut tribes, who lived just north of the Great Wall of China, had been entrusted with the defense of the Wall by the Chin. But the Onguts were friendly toward their Mongol cousins. In 1204, they had warned Genghis of the planned attack by the Naimans, and now they permitted the Mongol troops to pass the Great Wall. They also provided good grazing areas where the Mongols could rest after the trip across the Gobi Desert. To strengthen this alliance, Genghis had arranged marriages between his family and that of the Ongut khan.

Genghis sent one horde—probably Jebei's—on a raid against

* The city now known as Peking had been called Yen-ching by the Liao, and renamed Chung Tu by the Chin; Genghis Khan's grandson, Kublai Khan, would rename it Khanbahg; the new rulers of China, after they expelled the Mongols, renamed it Peking in 1409.

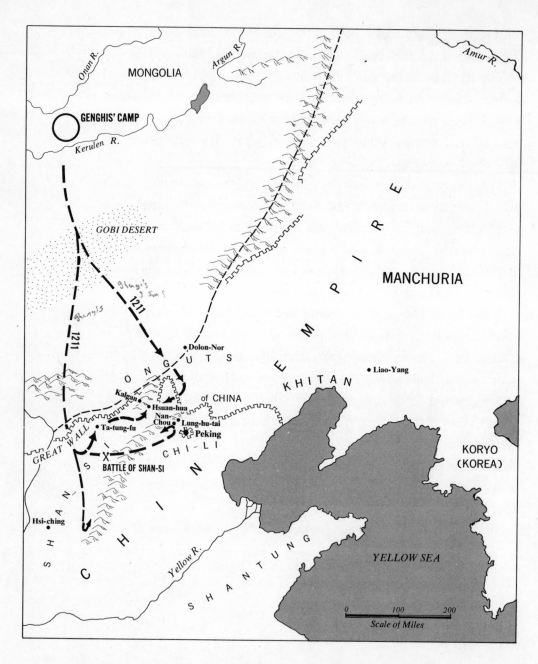

MONGOLIA

Onan R.

Argun R.

Amur R.

GENGHIS' CAMP

Kerulen R.

GOBI DESERT

MANCHURIA

Ghingis's Sun's

1211

Ghingis

1211

• Dolon-Nor

O N G U T S

of CHINA

KHITAN

• Liao-Yang

Kalgan •

Hsuan-hua •

Nan-
Chou •

Lung-hu-tai

• Peking

Ta-tung-fu •

GREAT WALL

CHI-LI

X
BATTLE OF SHAN-SI

S H A N S I

C H I N

KORYO
(KOREA)

• Hsi-ching

Yellow R.

S H A N T U N G

YELLOW SEA

0   100   200
Scale of Miles

The War against Chin, 1211–1215

Peking, while the main body of the army advanced into the northwestern province of Shan-si. This caught the Chin by surprise. They had expected the main Mongol attack to be against Peking, and had assembled an army of 500,000 near the capital. Now, after having been harassed by Jbei's hit-and-run raid, the Chin army had to march westward through mountain passes and into the plains of Shan-si, more than 200 miles to the west. Somewhere, between the mountains and the Yellow River, Genghis and his army were waiting. Apparently he attacked the Chinese before they were completely ready for battle, probably while they were still marching through the passes. In any event, in a few hours of slaughter he over-whelmed and destroyed the Chin army. The Mongols then began to devastate and plunder Shan-si, untroubled by any effective Chinese resistance. The local militia were mostly foot soldiers and were no match for the Mongol cavalry in mobility or fighting capabilities.

Genghis led his own horde to Ta-tung-fu, the Chin western capital. He laid seige to the walled city for a month but could not take it. Meanwhile, the hordes of Juji, Jagatai, and Ogatai devastated Shan-si Province, and then moved eastward through the mountains again to the province of Chi-li (or Hopeh). Meanwhile, Jebei's horde made a reconnaissance in force through the area around Peking, to get information about the passes leading to the plains around the capital city.

In Chi-li Province the Mongols continued to be thwarted in their efforts to take the strongly defended walled cities. They still could not handle a siege effectively. Jebei had better

37

results, and captured a few of the fortresses defending the passes leading to Peking. Then Genghis concentrated his other four hordes and they proceeded to Peking through the passes taken by Jebei.

Peking was the most strongly defended city of China. There were 18 miles of walls, 40 feet high and 40 feet across the top, 50 feet thick at the bottom. There were three moats surrounding the city and nine hundred towers. Just outside the walls there were four forts, each well defended and well supplied, covering the best approaches to the city.

The Mongol horses ran free on the plains around Peking, and no army appeared to dispute this area with the Mongol cavalry. But Genghis knew that it would be impossible for his forces to capture the city by assault, and he also knew that he could not supply his horses and men long enough to starve the city into surrender. He stayed for about a month in the plain until all the grass had been eaten by his horses, and then began to withdraw. The Chin emperor thought this would be a good time to seek peace with the Mongols and sent one of his generals as an ambassador to negotiate—and also to obtain information. But the Mongols learned more from the Chin ambassador—a general—than he did from them. The most important information that Genghis discovered was that the Liao princes in nearby Khitan were not loyal to the Chin. (Khitan is now southern Manchuria, a region between Peking and Korea on the Yellow Sea.) The peace negotiations failed, so Genghis headed north with all the forces for the winter of 1211–12. He sent emissaries ahead to Yo-lu Lin-ko, the Liao prince of Khitan, encouraging him to revolt against the Chin.

The Mongols crossed the Great Wall north of Peking. Here there were two parallel walls, with a long expanse of good grazing land between them. This was where the Chin raised horses for their cavalry. The Mongols captured the entire herd of mares and young horses. Taking the valuable horses with them, the Mongols camped over a broad area just north of the Great Wall. During the winter, Genghis kept up negotiations with the Liao prince of Khitan. At the same time he kept his soldiers busy practicing new methods of siegecraft.

In the spring of 1212, Khitan revolted against the Chin. Genghis sent Jebei with his horde to help the Liao fight the Chin near the Yellow Sea. With the remainder of his army, Genghis marched south and west into Shan-si again. Dividing his army into two parts, Genghis swept through the province. He again found that the fortresses had been repaired and that the area was much better defended than the previous year. So he concentrated his effort on besieging the city of Hsi-ching. In an effort to capture the city by assault, Genghis himself led a storming party. But he was wounded by an arrow and his troops were repulsed from the stout walls by the defenders. After this failure he led his army back to the north to practice siegecraft some more.

Jebei had better success in besieging the city of Liao-yang in Khitan. First, he tried an assault, and failed completely. He withdrew in a pretended hasty retreat, leaving many supplies and much of the army baggage before the walls. Then, after marching away for two days, Jebei led his troops back as fast as they could march, ready for battle. They found, as he had hoped, that the inhabitants as well as the defending garrison were outside the city, looting the deserted Mongol camp. The gates were open, the walls undefended. Sweeping across the plain the Mongols quickly took the town and slaughtered the garrison. Because of this success, the Liao were able to hold Khitan and declared themselves independent of the Chin, with Genghis Khan as overlord.

Mongol Siegecraft

By this time Genghis had finally developed a successful siege technique, after extensive analytical study, and repeated practice in training and combat. The resulting system for assaulting fortifications soon became well-nigh irresistible. An important element of this system was a large, but mobile, siege train, with missile engines and other equipment carried on wagons and pack animals. Genghis conscripted the best Chinese engineers to comprise the manpower of the siege train, and he adopted Chinese weapons, equipment, and techniques. Combining generous terms of service with threats and force, Genghis created an engineer corps at least as efficient as those of Alexander the Great and Caesar.

Important cities and fortifications would usually be invested by one touman—supported by all or part of the engineer train—while the main force marched onward. Sometimes by strategem, ruse, or bold assault, the town would be quickly stormed. If this proved impossible, the besieging touman and the engineers began regular siege operations, while the main army sought out the enemy's principal field forces. Once a Mongol victory had been achieved in the field, besieged towns and cities often surrendered without further resistance. In such cases, the inhabitants were treated with only moderate severity.

But if the defenders of a city or fort were foolish enough to attempt to defy the besiegers, Genghis' amazingly efficient engineers would soon create a breach in the walls, or prepare other methods for a successful assault by the dismounted toumans. Then the conquered city, its garrison, and its inhabitants would be subjected to the pillaging and destruction which have made the name of Genghis Khan one of the most feared in history.

Sometimes even the strongest cities were overwhelmed and captured before they were fully aware that any large force of Mongols was in their vicinity. The leading Mongol light-horsemen always attempted to pursue defeated enemies so closely and so vigorously as to ride through the city gates before these could be closed. Even if the enemy were sufficiently alert to prevent this, he rarely anticipated the speed, efficiency, and vigor with which the Mongol engines of war—Chinese ballistae and catapults—were put into action within a few minutes of the arrival of the leading cavalry units. The Mongols discovered that a prompt assault, covered by a hail of fire from these machines, would often permit them to scale the walls and to seize a portion of the defenses before the surprised enemy was prepared to resist.

If the initial assaults were repulsed and regular siege operations were required, then the ballistae and catapults provided fire cover for battering rams, siege towers, and all of the normal methods of siegecraft. When the Mongols were prepared to make their final major assault through a breach, or over the opposing fortifications, they frequently made use of a ruthless, heartless, but usually effective method of approach. Herding great numbers of helpless captives in front of them, the dismounted Mongol troopers would advance to the walls, forcing the defenders to kill their own countrymen in order to be able to bring fire against the attackers.

To add to the confusion and difficulties of the enemy, the Mongols often preceded their assaults by firing flaming arrows into besieged camps and cities to start fires. These arrows were fired by light cavalrymen dashing in front of the walls, as well as by catapults from farther away.

Mongol Staff and Command

It was during his campaigns against the Chin that Genghis Khan also perfected his system of command, and the staff structure which enabled him to exercise command. We know little of the details of this system, probably because the history of his operations was mostly written by his enemies, who rarely understood how he accomplished his victories. When he was in the field himself, he seems to have been his own operations officer, although he evidently made considerable use of the skill and genius of able subordinates like his four sons and Jebei and Sabutai. He encouraged them to learn command skills so that they could operate effectively without his personal presence.

Strategy and tactics for every Mongol campaign were obviously prepared in painstaking detail in advance. An essential element of the planning for these campaigns was Genghis' intelligence system. Operations plans were always based on thorough study and evaluation of amazingly complete and accurate information. In later years this Mongol intelligence network spread through the world; its thoroughness excelled all others of the Middle Ages. Spies generally operated under the guise of merchants or traders.

Once Genghis had evaluated the intelligence, he laid out general plans for the entire campaign. He assigned missions to the commanders of each horde or independent touman. He gave very wide latitude to each subordinate commander to accomplish his specific assigned objective in the way each one thought best. Prior to a general engagement, the touman commanders were at liberty to maneuver freely, and were required only to follow the general outlines of Genghis' overall campaign plan. Orders and the exchange of combat intelligence information passed rapidly between the Khan's headquarters and his subordinate units by the swift mounted messengers. Thus Genghis, even without radios and airplanes, was able to assure complete unity of command at all levels, and at the same time retain close personal control over operations extending over hundreds of miles.

The Mongols were particularly skillful in their psychological warfare. Tales of their ruthlessness, barbarity, and of the slaughter of obstinate foes, were spread about the countryside in a deliberate propaganda campaign. This discouraged resistance by the next intended victim. As a matter of fact, while there was considerable truth in this propaganda, it was equally true that the Mongols were very generous in their treatment of any enemy who cooperated, particularly those who had skills which the great Khan thought might be operationally or administratively useful.

Genghis used some of his best orlok as advisers, just like a modern general staff. This is shown by the way the Mongols responded to the lessons of their campaigns. They promptly analyzed the events of each of their major actions; then put the results of this analysis to work immediately in a systematic training program. This could have been possible only if Genghis was assisted by an alert, smoothly functioning staff.

Genghis left the problem of gathering supplies on campaign to individual subordinate commanders. The Mongol toumans lived off the country by means of a ruthless requisitioning procedure. It is clear that this was done efficiently and systematically, because of the uniform success of the Mongols in maintaining their forces, even when operating in desert and mountain regions. The administrative staff of the great Khan apparently consisted largely of captured Chinese scholars, officials, and surgeons who had been forcibly recruited during the campaigns against Hsi-Hsia and the early operations against the Chin.

We have already seen how Genghis made extensive use of couriers or messengers for long-range communications purposes. Tactical movements were controlled by black and white signal flags, under the direction of squadron and regimental commanders. Thus there were no delays caused by poorly written orders or messages. In fact, probably only a few of the Mongol commanders could read or write. The signal flags were particularly useful for coordinating the movements of units beyond the range of voice control.

When signal flags could not be seen, either because of darkness or intervening terrain features, the Mongols used flaming arrows for sending prearranged messages.

Third Campaign Against the Chin (1213)

The third campaign against the Chin Empire was launched by Genghis Khan in the spring of 1213, with grim determination to use his new system to capture defended fortresses and cities. He marched south across the Great Wall into the northern provinces, taking every fortress on the route. He soon was satisfied that his system was working and was pleased to find his soldiers becoming increasingly efficient in every siege and assault.

In July, 1213, Genghis led his army eastward along the Kalgan-Peking Road. This mountainous route was studded with easily defended passes and fortified towns. The main body bypassed the towns and attacked the passes. Behind them came the siege train, commanded by Genghis' youngest son, Tuli. Over a period of about a month the Mongols moved down the road toward Peking, capturing the walled towns of Hsuan-hua, Pau-an, and Huai-lai, one after the other.

The pass west of Nan-Chow was defended by a powerful Chin army. By feigning retreat, Genghis lured the Chins from the heights, then he turned and struck vigorously at the pursuing Chinese. We do not know the tactics he used, but probably the counterattack was a double envelopment. The Chin army was shattered, then crushed, with great loss of life. Then Genghis swept through the pass and beyond Nan-Chow to camp at Lung-hu-tai, at the edge of the great plains of northern China, close to Peking. It was early fall of 1213.

One portion of the Mongol army, meanwhile, had reoccupied northern Shan-si. It was then reported to Genghis that his ally, the Ongut khan, who had originally helped him into China, was threatened by a revolt. He immediately detached several toumans from his army and sent them northwest to help his friend and ally. Soon the revolt was suppressed, and the toumans returned. Genghis, who had halted his offensive against Peking, now moved closer to the city.

This diversionary expedition to the Ongut lands was an interesting demonstration of the loyalty of Genghis Khan to those who were loyal to him. This quality undoubtedly was one of the principal reasons for the complete dedication he received in return from his warriors, from his tribal chiefs, and from his faithful allies.

46

The presence of the Mongol hordes so near Peking naturally caused chaos in the city and completely disrupted the government. In a palace revolution, Emperor Wei-Wang was overthrown and murdered by his senior general, Hu-Sha-hu, who installed the crown prince as the new Emperor Hsuan-tsung. But Hu-Sha-hu himself actually seized the reigns of government as a dictator.

As soon as he had established his authority in Peking, Hu-Sha-hu ordered another general, Kao-chi, to take the Chin army out of the city to attack the Mongols. But by this time their many defeats at the hands of the Mongols had reduced the confidence and morale of the Chinese soldiers. A halfhearted Chin sortie was easily repulsed by Genghis Khan, and Kao-chi feared that Hu-Sha-hu would have him executed for failure. So only a few weeks after Hu-Sha-hu had seized power, the defeated general himself decided to rebel against the dictator. He slew Hu-Sha-hu and then presented his head to Emperor Hsuan-tsung.

The grateful emperor thereupon appointed Kao-chi to be commander of the imperial forces. The new commanding general knew that he could not defeat the Mongols in the field, but he believed he could keep them from capturing Peking. He began an energetic effort to strengthen the city's defenses.

Genghis Khan had taken advantage of the confusion in Peking to launch a devastating campaign of destruction through all of north China—the entire realm of the Chin. He again divided the Mongol army into five hordes. The three under Juji, Jagatai, and Ogatai went to plunder those portions of Shan-si that had not previously been devasted. Another horde, under Kasar, headed east into southern Manchuria, in the area between Khitan and Korea. Genghis led the fifth horde, accompanied by Tuli, and headed south into Shantung. The Mongol forces spent the fall and winter pillaging, looting, burning, and ravaging the countryside of all north China.

Genghis had three good reasons for this seemingly senseless pillage. In the first place, he wanted to find new grazing lands for his horses. Secondly, he wanted his troops to continue practicing their siege techniques. Finally, he wanted to weaken the entire Chin Empire so that no assistance would be sent to Peking.

During this six-month period the Mongols took ninety fortified towns. They killed thousands of the inhabitants and herded many more with them as prisoners to perform various kinds of labor while they traveled over the country of the Chin.

Genghis soon found that the terror created by these methods was a very effective weapon, and prevented later victims from offering effective resistance. He also found, however, that the disease and famine which resulted from the devastation were sometimes harmful to his troops. But his men were hardy, and they could always move from stricken regions, leaving the poor Chinese to suffer and die from starvation and pestilence.

The Mongols took much booty during this winter campaign. They deposited this with their Ongut allies during the spring, and then all five hordes returned to Peking. In April, 1214, they again camped in the plains near the great city.

Fourth Campaign Against the Chin (1214)

The four forts just outside the walls of Peking were easily taken with the newly perfected siege techniques and engines of war. But two attempts to take the city itself failed, in spite of intensive use of the catapults and ballistae with which the Mongols were now expert. Genghis Khan did not attempt a third assault—his losses had been too heavy. Furthermore, he had heard rumors that the Chin and the people of Peking were weary of the siege; the whole population was desperate for peace.

Genghis sent an emissary, a Tangut, to Emperor Hsuan-tsung, suggesting a truce. His message to the Chin emperor is recorded in the Chinese histories: ". . . You have only Peking left. God has made you impotent, but if I press you harder, I do not know what Heaven would say. I am willing to withdraw my army, but what provisions will you make to satisfy my generals?"

When the Chin emperor read this, he realized that he would have to pay a stiff price for peace. After listening to the advice of his courtiers and generals, Hsuan-tsung decided to pay the price. In May of 1214 a peace treaty was signed. The Chin recognized the independence of the Liao princes in Khitan. Much more important was the emperor's gift to Genghis of his sister, Princess Chi-kuo, as a bride; this signified Hsuan-tsung's acceptance of Genghis Khan as overlord of the Chin domains. With her, Princess Chi-kuo brought a train of five hundred young children, three thousand horses, and much gold and silk. Vast quantities of gold and silver were also given to the Mongols to divide among the officers and men.

After this arrangement the Mongols departed from Peking with their booty and crossed the Great Wall, taking with them a leading Chin general, Wan-Yen Fu-Hsing, as a hostage. They also brought thousands of their Chinese prisoners, most of whom were forced to serve in the siege train. At the edge of the Gobi Desert the army camped for a while at Dolon-nor. There Genghis released Wan-Yen Fu-Hsing and let him return to Peking, but he ordered that all prisoners who had no particular skills or usefulness in the siege train, or in the newly established engineer corps, should be killed.

Genghis was apparently satisfied with what he had accomplished in northern China. We do not know whether he harbored any ambition to return to humble further or to conquer the Chin, but it is probable that he did not. If he had been thinking of expanded conquests, he probably would not have concluded peace with the Chin emperor in 1214, but would have pressed his advantage until the Chins were completely overwhelmed.

The Chin Revival

While men and horses were still resting at Dolon-nor, in July of 1214, Genghis received word that Hsuan-tsung had left Peking and had moved his court to Kai-feng fu, a large city in the province of Honan, on the Yellow River. He had left Crown Prince Shu-hsu and General Wan-Yen Fu-Hsing in charge of Peking, with orders to strengthen the defenses and to be prepared to withstand future Mongol attacks. The Chin emperor was evidently determined to regain his independence from Genghis.

At this time Genghis also received a messenger from the Sung emperor, appealing for support. The ruler of south China was worried by this move of the Chin court to Kai-feng fu, so near the boundary between the Chin and Sung dominions. Soon after this, Genghis also learned that a Chin army had been sent from Peking to reconquer the Liao kingdom of Khitan.

Genghis was now faced with a very difficult decision. He had been away from Mongolia for more than three years, and felt that he should get back to his empire to make certain that affairs were in order there. He was probably particularly worried by reports of border troubles in the west and southwest of Mongolia. He was also concerned lest Hsi-Hsia and Kara-Khitai, and other enemies in central Asia, would take advantage of his long absence to regain the lands he had conquered in previous years.

Yet at the same time Genghis felt that it would be a mistake to let the Chin rebuild their strength for a later war. This would mean that the efforts he had made, and the losses he had suffered, in the previous three years would all be wasted. The strength and population of north China were still tremendous, and if the Chin were to make an all-out effort to mobilize this strength, Genghis feared that he might be worsted in a later campaign. Furthermore, as a man of honor, he could not let the Chin break the treaty and reconquer Khitan from his Liao allies.

After deliberating about these matters, Genghis again divided his army in four hordes. One of these he kept at Dolon-nor, which became his temporary capital and headquarters. From that central point he could supervise the far-flung operations which he now planned. He sent one horde, under Sabutai, to operate in northern Manchuria, ancestral home of the Chin rulers, to create terror, to inflict punishment, and generally to prevent the country from recovering from the devastation of previous campaigns. Mukuli was sent with the second horde to give direct assistance to the Liao in Khitan. A smaller force, under Jebei, was sent back to Mongolia to make certain that the home base remained calm, stable, and orderly. Apparently Genghis kept his four sons with him, as part of his general staff.

During the fall and early winter of 1214 Sabutai carried destruction across northern Manchuria and then marched south into Korea. The Korean monarch quickly swore allegiance to Genghis. Meanwhile, Mukuli helped the Liao repulse the Chin invaders, then pursued and drove them from the entire area of central and southern Manchuria. There must have been cooperation between Sabutai and Mukuli in these operations, but we know nothing of the details.

During the winter, in the meantime, the Chin crown prince and General Wan-Yen Fu-Hsing were hurriedly rebuilding Chin military power in north China and strengthening the fortifications of Peking. The outer defenses of the city were restored in two months. This vigorous leadership restored the shaken morale of the Chin army. But when Emperor Hsuan-tsung sent for the crown prince to come to the new capital, Kai-feng fu, the people of Peking became discouraged, fearing that the Chin dynasty had decided to abandon the city to the Mongols. The arrival of a Mongol touman from Mukuli's army outside the city walls in September added to the unrest and discouragement of the people. General Wan-Yen held out during the winter, and although the Mongols took many other towns and cities in northern China, they could not capture Peking itself.

Final Campaigns Against the Chin

Several relief armies were sent by the Chin emperor from his new capital in the south, but Mukuli, who had now taken command outside Peking, easily repulsed these. In the spring, gallant Wan-Yen decided on a desperate sortie, and asked the other generals to die with him in a last effort to save Peking. But the Chin generals refused, and most of them fled to safety. Wan-Yen then disposed of all his possessions, following which he committed suicide in the midst of growing chaos within the city.

In May of 1215, shortly after Wan-Yen's death, Mukuli took Peking with only 5,000 Mongols and a contingent of Khitan allies. The Mongols and Khitans set fire to the city, while they seized anything worth taking. In addition to rich loot—silks, jewels, and silver—they also took human beings who were skilled craftsmen and sent them along with the endless caravans of treasure to Genghis' camp on Lake Dolon-nor. Among these prisoners was a Liao prince, Yeliu-Chutsai, a scholar and scientist who had been serving the Chin government. Genghis talked with Yeliu and was greatly impressed by his wisdom and ability. Believing Yeliu to be trustworthy, the Khan immediately appointed this Chinese official to a position of trust as his adviser on the administration of the newly conquered provinces of north China. Eventually Yeliu was to become virtual prime minister of the Mongol Empire.

After the fall of Peking the Mongol armies moved south into the heart of the Chin territory. Apparently Genghis remained at Dolon-nor for another two years, supervising the conquest of the Chin, and keeping a close eye on affairs in Mongolia. Probably he himself visited his field armies and made trips to Mongolia, but the records are incomplete and we do not know much about this period in Genghis' life. Evidently much of his attention was devoted to organizing the administration of the vast new regions his armies were conquering. Most of the provinces were placed under Liao governors from Khitan. Following the advice of Yeliu-Chutsai, Genghis established a system for levying regular taxes rather than making systematic raids upon conquered territories as had been the Mongol custom. This was the beginning of a system of military government that Genghis and Yeliu perfected in later years.

After Genghis had completed these administrative arrangements for his new provinces, he placed Mukuli in charge of all continuing operations in China in September, 1217. Mukuli was given complete authority as the viceroy of the Khan. The troops remaining in China—evidently two toumans of Mongols and about 20,000 Khitans—were told that Mukuli's commands must be obeyed as though he were the Khakan himself. Then Genghis Khan left China, never to return.

CHAPTER 5

War in the West

Turmoil in Central Asia

To the west and southwest of Mongolia lay that vast part of central Asia now known as Turkestan. Most of the northeastern portion of the region was the large kingdom of Kara-Khitai (including modern Chinese Turkestan and that portion of Siberia around Lake Balkhash). This kingdom had been founded by a fugitive Liao prince after the Chin took north China from the Liao dynasty a century earlier. Although the rulers were now Chinese or Khitans, most of the people of Kara-Khitai were Turkish, and the Moslem religion predominated. It was essentially an agricultural society, unlike that of the nomadic Mongols.

The Uighur nation, another Turkish people, lay northeast of Kara-Khitai, southwest of Mongolia, and west of Hsi-Hsia. The Uighurs were the earliest civilized Turks, whose culture and alphabet had been adopted by many other central Asian peoples, including the Naimans, and then by all the Mongols. In 1211 the Uighur leader, Barchuq, had sent gifts to Genghis Khan, recognizing him as the ruler of Mongolia. In turn Genghis sent

56

Barchuq a Mongol princess for wife. Relations between the Uighurs and the Mongols continued to be friendly. But Barchuq became increasingly worried by threats from Kara-Khitai, and by events occurring in the Liao kingdom.

For several years Kara-Khitai had been in turmoil. Guchluk, the son of the dead Naiman ruler who had fled from Genghis and Juji into Kara-Khitai in 1208, had been given refuge by King Yelu-cheluku. Soon after this Guchluk married the king's daughter. But in 1211, Guchluk imprisoned Yelu-cheluku and seized control of Kara-Khitai. He soon became extremely unpopular with his subjects because he persecuted the Moslem religion, and because he was ruthless in suppressing all opposition to his rule. Guchluk's oppressive rule led some of his vassals to send gifts to his old enemy Genghis Khan, even though Guchluk brutally killed anyone who committed such an act of treason. He also began to make threats against the Uighurs, and this was what Barchuq was worried about.

Soon after Genghis returned to Karakorum, in 1217, he decided that he should try to restore stability in Kara-Khitai, and to help the people who had asked him to liberate them from the cruel rule of Guchluk. This would also end the threat to his Uighur ally, Barchuq. Late that year Genghis ordered Jebei to take a horde to Kara-Khitai and to capture and kill Guchluk. Jebei's instructions were to leave the population unmolested and not to plunder the kingdom, but to annex it to the Mongol Empire.

When Jebei's Mongols entered Kara-Khitai, early in 1218, the people welcomed them as liberators, and the leaders of all the frontier provinces promptly recognized Genghis Khan's over-lordship. Jebei made the Mongols even more popular by opening all the mosques, and stopping the religious persecution of Guchluk. All religions were put on an equal footing and all given complete tolerance, which made the Moslems flock to Mongol protection.

As Jebei approached Kashgar, Guchluk's capital, the king fled to the Pamir Mountains. Jebei pursued Guchluk relentlessly across the "Roof of the World," and captured him in the 10,000-foot valley of Sary-kol. He immediately had the fallen king put to death.

The conquest of Kara-Khitai had taken only a few weeks. Jebei sent Guchluk's head, along with one thousand white-muzzled horses—for which the country was famed—back to Genghis. The Khakan was well pleased by what Jebei had accomplished, but he sent back a message that Jebei should not become too proud because of his rapid victories. He also ordered Jebei to conquer the mountain tribes farther west (between modern Chinese and Russian Turkestan) to secure the frontiers of his new dominions. Jebei quickly accomplished the task.

The Merkits who inhabited the region north of Kara-Khitai were traditional enemies of the Mongols, and had aided Guchluk in the brief war. So, while Jebei was consolidating Kara-Khitai, Genghis sent Juji and Sabutai to invade the Merkit territory. They soon subjugated the Merkit tribes, then went farther west to obtain the submission of the overawed Kipchaks west of the Irtysh River and north of the Aral Sea.

The Khwarizmian Empire

Beyond the mountain frontier subdued by Jebei there was a powerful new empire. Ala-ed-din Mohammed, Turkish Shah of Khwarizm, had reestablished and expanded the ancient Persian Empire. His territories included most of the regions now known as Iran, Russian Turkestan, Afghanistan, and Pakistan. He kept his capital in Samarkand, in Transoxiana, the heart of the Khwarizmian Empire.

Although there had been some evidence that Guchluk had been allied with Shah Mohammed, Genghis appears not to have harbored any resentment, nor to have had any ambition to go to war against Khwarizm or to conquer any of its territory. In 1217 he sent ambassadors to Samarkand, with a message for the Shah:

"I send thee greeting. I know thy power and the vast extent of thine empire; I regard thee as my most cherished son. On my part, thou must know that I have conquered China and all the Turkish nations north of it. Thou knowest that my country is a magazine of warriors, a mine of silver, and that I have no need of other lands. I take it that we have an equal interest in encouraging trade between our subjects."

Shah Mohammed seems to have accepted this peaceful message in the spirit in which it was obviously intended. A treaty of commerce was signed between the two empires late in 1217. The ancient silk route from the Mediterranean to China passed through Khwarizm and thence through Kara-Khitai to Hsi-Hsia and China. The treaty provided for free passage of trade across the frontiers of the two powerful new empires. For a while the treaty was satisfactory to both parties.

In 1218 Shah Mohammed began a campaign to conquer Mesopotamia. Caliph Nasir of Bagdad, together with the Nestorian Christian Patriarch of Bagdad, sent a messenger to Genghis asking his help, suggesting that he should invade the Shah's territory from the east, while Mohammed's troops were advancing west toward Bagdad. Genghis replied: "I am not at war with him."

Shah Mohammed brought back his army without reaching Bagdad, however. His troops could not endure the extreme cold of the Iranian highlands—near the Persian Gates, where Alexander had fought a winter campaign fifteen centuries before. Furthermore, when Mohammed learned that the Mongols had overrun Kara-Khitai, he was concerned about his northeastern frontier and decided to concentrate all his troops in and around Transoxiana. He moved his court back to Samarkand.

It was about this time that Mohammed learned that the governor of the border fortress of Otrar had captured a Mongol caravan in which he had discovered three Mongol spies. Mohammed sent orders to Otrar to kill the spies. The greedy governor, who wanted the treasures of the caravan, killed all of the people with the caravan—about 150—and took everything. A single slave escaped and got word of the massacre to Genghis.

Genghis assumed that the governor of Otrar was responsible for the killing of the Mongol merchants, so he sent an ambassador to Shah Mohammed, asking that the governor be sent to him for punishment. But the Shah, angered by Genghis' request, had the Mongol ambassador killed, and sent back the other two members of the embassy with their beards shaved. This was a mortal insult, a virtual declaration of war. Genghis thereupon sent messengers to all of his vassals, telling them what had happened, and requesting that they provide troops for the coming war.

Until this time all of the evidence indicates that Genghis Khan had truly meant the peaceful words of his message to Shah Mohammed in 1217. He seems to have been completely satisfied with what he had conquered, and to have had no further territorial ambitions. If this is so, then the incident at Otrar was one of the most momentous accidents of history. The senseless massacre of the Mongol traders started a train of events that was to lead to the Mongol conquest of Persia, which in turn was to result in Mongol invasions of Europe, and their subsequent conquest of all of eastern Europe. It was also the direct cause of a renewed Mongol invasion of Hsi-Hsia, which in turn was to lead to Mongol conquest of the remaining territories of the Chin Empire and of the Sung Empire of north China.

When Genghis sent out a request to his vassals to supply troops for the war with Khwarizm, all responded at once, and sent troops as asked, with one exception. The king of Hsi-Hsia refused. He replied that if Genghis could not punish the Shah with his own forces, he should not be Khakan. Genghis remembered this reply, and later did something about it—action that resulted directly in the eventual Mongol conquest of all China. But for the moment he concentrated all his attention on the war against Khwarizm.

In the late spring of 1219 the Mongol army assembled in Uighur territory on the upper Irtysh River. It was the largest army Genghis ever assembled: about 200,000 warriors, plus a complete engineer and siege train, including catapults and flamethrowers. From his efficient spy system Genghis knew that the Shah's forces totaled about 400,000 troops.

Juji's and Jebei's Raid

Meanwhile Genghis had sent his son Juji to join Jebei in an advance from Kara-Khitai into Khwarizm from the east. Juji and Jebei had two missions. First they were to distract the Khwarizmians from the planned assembly of the main Mongol armies far to the north. Second, they were to reconnoiter eastern Khwarizm.

Jebei and the prince left Kashgar in the early spring of 1219 with a force of 25,000 to 30,000 men. They crossed the lofty Tien Shan Mountains through a pass 13,000 feet high, filled with snow 5 feet and more deep. To protect their horses from the cold, the soldiers wrapped their legs in yak skins, but many animals and men died. They ran out of food during the rugged march and were forced to eat dead animals. Finally they descended into the Fergana Valley of the Syr-Darya to find spring in full bloom and rich pastureland for their horses. But also in the valley, east of Khojend, the exhausted Mongols discovered a large contingent of the Shah's troops, about 50,000 men, fresh and completely equipped for battle, under the Shah's son, Jelal ed-Din.

Juji and Jebei decided to withdraw toward the mountains, apparently hoping to lead the Khwarizmians into an ambush. The result was a desperate and inconclusive battle near Fergana. There is a Mongol legend that Juji and Jelal ed-Din were each almost captured by the opposing side, but were saved by strenuous efforts of loyal soldiers. The Mongols withdrew to the mountains in the night following this battle. The Khwarizmians, happy to see them go, made no effort to follow.

Jebei sent a messenger to Genghis, reporting what had happened. Genghis sent a return message, ordering Jebei and Juji to move south of Kashgar to the upper Amu-Darya, where large reinforcements would join them. Juji was then to ride down this river with his horde, then march westward toward Samarkand and Bukhara. Jebei was to continue down the river and attack Transoxiana from the south.

Invasion of Khwarizm

Soon after he sent this message to Jebei, probably early July of 1219, Genghis and the main body of the Mongol army left the Irtysh River. He divided his army into four hordes, about four or five toumans each. One of these hordes, as promised, was to go to the upper Amu-Darya, where Juji would take command. Jagatai and Ogatai were to march southwest toward Otrar with two hordes. Genghis himself led about 50,000 men in a wide westward swing through the desert, planning to advance against Bukhara from the west. He hoped to confuse and surprise the Khwarizmians by these widespread attacks from four different directions.

As planned, Jagatai and Ogatai suddenly appeared at Otrar, the fortress near the border between the Khwarizmian Empire and Kara-Khitai where the governor had murdered the members of the Mongol caravan. The Turks at Otrar fought with the knowledge that none would be spared. The siege lasted for five months, before the Mongols finally broke through the walls. They spread out through the city in search of the governor, finding him at last on a roof, all of his arrows expended, and hurling tiles because he was out of ammunition. They captured him alive, but every other member of the garrison was killed or enslaved. The governor was sent to Genghis, who had molten silver poured into his eyes and ears, and then had him tortured to death.

Meanwhile Juji had joined his horde on the upper Amu-Darya, as ordered by Genghis. Then, following Genghis' plan, he advanced separately from Jebei, marching directly on Khojend, on the Syr-Darya. The Mongols stormed into the town, but the governor, Timur Melik, fled to a fortress in the middle of the river, which he held with about one thousand warriors. Mongol assaults by boat were driven off. So Juji built a causeway into

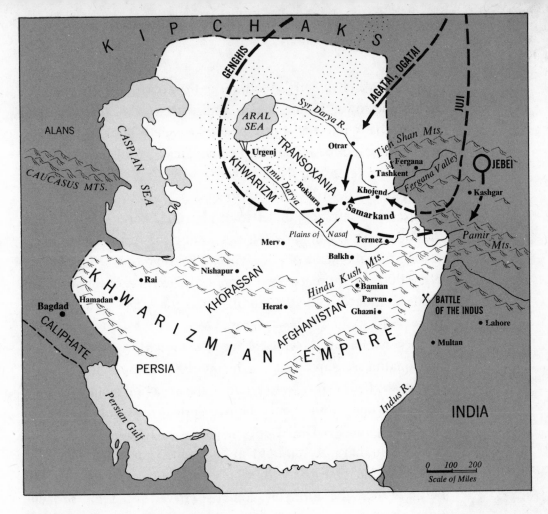

Invasion of the Khwarizmian Empire, 1220

the river, while Melik fired at the Mongols with catapults and sent out bowmen in boats to interfere with the construction.

When Timur realized that Juji's causeway was about to reach to the fortress, he and his men escaped in several boats. They fled down the river, breaking a chain which the Mongols had stretched across the river in the hope of capturing them. Below the town, Timur landed, and with a small force escaped by horseback into the south, where he joined Jelal ed-Din, who was raising reinforcements in Persia. The story of the brave and resourceful defense of the river fortress by Timur was written and celebrated by both Turks and Mongols.

After Juji left him, Jebei took his small horde—now barely 20,000 men—south and then west along the Amu-Darya, penetrating into the heart of Khwarizm. The Shah sent a detachment of 50,000 men to meet him. There is no account of the resultant battle, but Jebei's small army defeated the larger Khwarizmian force.

Shah Mohammed, who had been confident of the numerical and qualitative superiority of his 400,000 troops, had made a deadly strategic error. Not certain of the direction from which the Mongol attack would come, he had spread his troops along the frontier of the Syr-Darya and in garrisons to protect the large towns—Bukhara, Samarkand, and Urgenj. Thus he had no major concentration of force with which he could fight an offensive battle. When the Mongols actually arrived on a far broader front—and from more directions—than he had expected, the Shah seems to have panicked. From then on he thought only of escape for himself and his family.

Conquest of Transoxiana

The biggest surprise to Shah Mohammed was when Genghis himself appeared at Bukhara in February of 1220, marching from the west. Not only was this from a direction in which no threat had been foreseen, but it seemed impossible that the Mongols could have crossed a 400-mile stretch of desert with no life or forage. The surprised garrison of Bukhara—about 20,000 to 30,000 Turkish warriors—were thunderstruck. Most of them fled, trying to escape to the river. But they were followed by the Mongols who killed or captured nearly all. The townspeople, who were Persian and devout Moslems, surrendered at once, accepting Genghis and his Mongols as the punishment of God. They gave the Mongols everything they demanded and even helped them to capture the citadel where the last Turkish defenders were all killed. Genghis ordered destruction of the walls and all of the important buildings of the town. It was left in such a state that it could not easily be rebuilt into a defensive bastion against the Mongols after they had ridden on to the south and east.

Genghis had hoped to find the Shah at Bukhara. Disappointed to discover that the Shah was not there, Genghis went on toward Samarkand, where he again hoped for an opportunity to capture Mohammed. He was convinced that once the Shah was overthrown, Khwarizmian resistance would collapse.

Samarkand, Mohammed's capital, was a city of culture and commerce with over 500,000 inhabitants. It was also the strongest fortress of the realm, and here the Shah had hastily gathered a force of more than 100,000 Turkish soldiers. Genghis Khan arrived outside Samarkand in March and was soon joined by the other Mongol armies: Juji, with his army from Khajend in the east; Jebei who had defeated the Shah's forces in the south; and Jagatai and Ogatai fresh from the capture of Otrar in the north.

In amazement townspeople and garrison watched from the walls and towers as the Mongol hordes gathered from all points of the compass. Prisoners with the hordes were made to march in file with standards and the townspeople thought these were also Mongol soldiers. Thus they considerably overestimated the size of the Mongol forces, which in fact totaled less than 200,000 men.

Shortly after his arrival, Genghis learned that the Shah was not in the city, but had fled when the Mongol armies were approaching. Genghis directed Jebei, Sabutai, and Toguchar (his son-in-law) to take 30,000 men—one touman each—to chase Mohammed down. He ordered these specially selected orlok to follow the Shah anywhere, "wherever he goes. Spare every town which surrenders, but destroy ruthlessly anyone who resists." Early in April, 1220, the three leaders set off on their mission.

Genghis now invested the city. The Khwarizmians had been convinced that the city could hold out for at least a year; it fell in three days. This was largely because of the absence of the Shah or any leader of courage and ability, and because of the terror the Mongols had created. The garrison attempted one sally, but when this failed, 30,000 of them deserted. The Mongols accepted this mass surrender, but several days later they killed all of the deserters because they never trusted traitors. The rest of the garrison retreated to the citadel, and the townspeople opened the gates of the city to the Mongols.

The Mongols gave favored treatment to the members of a

religious sect whose leader had led opposition to Shah Mohammed. These people were allowed to stay in their home, but the rest of the inhabitants were driven out into the plains while the Mongols looted the city and assaulted the citadel. The citadel soon fell and the garrison was slaughtered. The Mongols then impressed 60,000 men—artisans, craftsmen, and strong young laborers—to accompany the army. Apparently the remainder of the inhabitants were allowed to buy back their freedom, and were permitted to return to the city. Genghis appointed a leading member of the religious sect to be viceroy of the city; then the Mongol armies left.

Genghis Khan and his army camped for the summer of 1220 on the plains of Nasaf, south of Samarkand. This was an extremely pleasant mountain plateau, with woods, orchards, and parks, and cool mountain breezes. The encampment area extended nearly the distance from Samarkand to Bukhara, with the troops separated so that their horses could find good grazing land. Here the new Turkish and Persian recruits were trained in Mongol military methods. Ogatai devoted himself to improving the army's artillery—catapults and ballistae—on the basis of experience gained in the siege of Otrar.

Mongol Military Government

By this time, with the assistance of Yeliu-Chutsai, Genghis had perfected a system of government and control of conquered territory. This was probably the most carefully planned military government system to appear before the twentieth century. It was applied for the first time in Transoxiana and became the pattern for all future Mongol military government.

Once armed resistance ceased, the Mongols changed immediately from apparently wanton destruction to carefully calculated reconstruction. The civil administration was usually left under a local leader satisfactory to the Mongols, who was supported, and closely supervised, by a small Mongol occupation force. A census was taken and efficient tax-collection machinery was immediately established. Genghis Khan had no intention of allowing conquered territories to be a burden on his economy. On the contrary, the funds collected in this fashion not only maintained the local government and its occupation troops, but also were used to pay tributes to the Khakan.

The Mongols absolutely forbade any continuation of local and internal squabbles in their conquered territory. Law and order were rigidly and ruthlessly maintained. As a consequence, regimented conquered regions were usually far more peaceful under the Mongol occupation than they had been before the invasion.

Transoxiana became secure in the religious toleration which the Mongols practiced, and which they enforced in all newly conquered provinces. People went about their daily business again, confident that the Mongol conquest, after its initial death and terror, had brought them peace and security.

Pursuit of Shah Mohammed

Meanwhile, Jebei, Sabutai, and Toguchar had followed Shah Mohammed from Samarkand to Balkh, in the foothills of the Hindu Kush mountains. The Mongol troopers crossed the Amu-Darya by hanging to their horses' tails and floating their equipment along behind. At Balkh, they discovered that the Shah had left a few weeks earlier. The inhabitants eagerly offered to surrender. In accordance with Genghis' orders that they should do everything possible to separate the Shah from his subjects, the Mongol leaders left the city unmolested and they promptly followed the route taken by the Shah.

Other cities, including Herat and Merv, also surrendered without a struggle, and Jebei and Sabutai left them untouched. Toguchar, however, allowed his men to pillage a town which had surrendered to Jebei. Although Toguchar was the son-in-law of Genghis, Jebei was overall commander of the expedition. He reduced Toguchar to the rank of a private in the touman of Sabutai. Jebei evidently sent a message to Genghis to report what he had done, and Genghis approved. Orders had to be obeyed by all men of the army, whatever their rank or their kinship.

The Shah now decided to flee to Khorassan, where he hoped the people would be more loyal to his cause. But the Mongol policy was succeeding, and Khorassan did not offer him much safety or refuge. He continued southwest to Nishapur and from here sent for his mother, telling her to join him and to bring his harem from Urgenj. It was at Nishapur that, for the first time, he heard of the Mongol pursuit. He hastily left Nishapur and headed west.

71

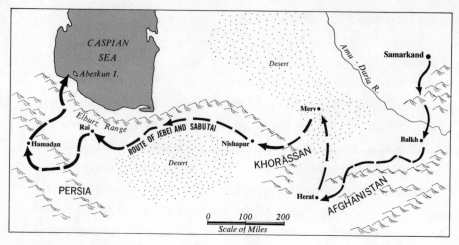

The Pursuit of Mohammed Shah, 1220–1221

Jebei and Sabutai reached Nishapur three weeks after the Shah had fled. When the city shut its gates to them, they assaulted it, but were repulsed, Toguchar being killed in an attempt to scale the walls. Jebei and Sabutai wanted vengeance, but they did not tarry to besiege Nishapur. Their mission was to pursue and capture the Shah.

By this time Shah Mohammed had ceased to plan for the defense of his empire. His only thought was to escape. In several Persian cities, armies were offered to him, but he was indecisive and unable to command them. His plans changed from day to day, as he moved westward through northern Persia. Jebei and Sabutai captured the Shah's mother, harem, and treasures, which they sent to Genghis. The small Mongol horde continued to pursue, following Shah Mohammed through the heart of his empire. A Persian army of 30,000 attempted to oppose them near pres-

72

ent-day Teheran at the city of Rai. The Mongols quickly defeated the Persians, then assaulted and sacked the town, massacring all of the inhabitants.

Near Hamadan the Mongols caught up with the Shah. The small force of Khwarizmians and Persians attempted to fight but were quickly scattered. Although Shah Mohammed was wounded, he escaped, and headed northward toward the Caspian Sea, closely followed by Jebei and Sabutai. He planned to take refuge on the island of Abeskun until his son, Jelal ed-Din could raise an army and come to his rescue. The Mongols followed him and saw his boat leaving the shore but did not know what became of him after that.

Jebei and Sabutai ruefully reported to Genghis that the Shah had escaped. They also sent back a train full of treasures they had taken in the pursuit. They camped on the shores of the Caspian, reconnoitering the area, and awaiting orders from Genghis.

Several months later the Mongols learned that the Shah had died on the island, in January of 1221, exhausted from the nine-month chase. Shah Mohammed was a weak man, who had collapsed completely after his initial overwhelming ambition and arrogance had been challenged.

CHAPTER 6

Conquest of Khwarizm, Khorassan, and Turkestan

Internal Squabbles

In the fall of 1220, Genghis took some of the Mongol forces to attack Termez on the Amu-Darya. Here he planned to test the improved siege equipment and artillery methods worked out by Ogatai. He wanted to make certain that the procedures were effective before sending the Mongol armies against Khwarizm, the original province of the Shah.

Termez was taken after a siege of eleven days. The inhabitants were treated cruelly; some were massacred, the remainder divided among the Mongols for slaves. Then Genghis set up a field headquarters for directing winter operations. He sent Juji, Jagatai, Ogatai, and Bogurchi with 50,000 men to take Urgenj, the capital city of the province of Khwarizm. The remainder of the army, now less than 100,000 men, he kept with him near Termez.

While waiting for reports from his detached sons and generals, Genghis organized a huge hunt of lions, wolves, leopards, and wild boar. The purpose was to occupy his troops and to keep them from becoming soft and quarrelsome. The Mongol hunt was a training ground for war; they encircled the wild animals just as they did cities, and the army practiced its fighting skills. This hunt lasted for four months.

Meanwhile, outside Urgenj, Juji and Jagatai were quarreling about leadership of the expedition. This delayed the siege of the city, giving the defenders time to prepare themselves. Although the dispute was not settled, the brothers finally turned to the task of capturing Urgenj. They could not use their siege equipment effectively because there were no stones in the area to provide ammunition for the catapults. As a substitute they put prisoners to work chopping down and cutting up trees, and they put prisoners to work filling in the moat, which took ten days. During this time, their dispute continued. Finally Bogurchi sent word to Genghis Khan about the state of affairs between the two princes.

Genghis immediately sent severe reprimands to his two elder sons and appointed their younger brother, Ogatai, over both of them. Ogatai then pressed the siege of Urgenj in a very resourceful fashion. To clear the defenders from the walls he used flames produced from naphtha or petroleum, a weapon adopted from the Mohammedans. Once a foothold was gained on the wall, the Mongols took the city, house by house, and street by street. The garrison and population resisted stubbornly for seven days, but finally, hemmed into a small area in the center of the city, they at last surrendered and asked for mercy. The Mongols showed them none, for they had been enraged by the bitter struggle and by the loss of their companions who fell in the fight. They led the surviving inhabitants outside the city, took women and children for slaves, set aside the craftsmen, and ruthlessly slaughtered the remaining male population, each Mongol warrior killing about twenty-four people. When this was done, they broke the dikes of the Amu-Darya and flooded the city. It was April, 1221.

Genghis was still provoked with his two elder sons for their quarreling. As a result Juji left the army, going into his own domains in the steppes of Kazakstan. Also, some other chiefs, including the Uighurs, wished to leave and return to their own peoples, now that the loss of the Mongol caravan had been revenged. Genghis allowed them to leave. This reduced his total army to about 100,000 men, besides the 30,000 soldiers of Sabutai and Jebei camped beside the Caspian.

Sabutai's Visit

Genghis now pondered about his future course of action. He sent for Sabutai since he wanted to get a firsthand report about the lands of west Khorassan through which Sabutai had ridden after the Shah. Genghis also wanted the advice of this brilliant young general, since he had not yet decided on a plan for future operations. Although the Khwarizmian Empire had collapsed, the Mongols had occupied only part of it. Afghanistan was particularly worrisome, since Genghis had received reports that Jelal ed-Din was raising a new army there.

When Sabutai received the order to report to Genghis, he wrapped himself in bandages, like the arrow messengers, and in

one week rode 1,200 miles to the Khakan's headquarters. There
he told Genghis in detail about Khorassan and also about northern Iraq, through which his touman had ridden. He assured
Genghis that it would be impossible for the Turkish Moslem
forces from the south and west to unite or to work together.
He was certain that the western Persians would not try to reconquer Khorassan or do anything to help Jelal ed-Din.

Genghis was relieved by Sabutai's information and opin-
ions. He decided that the forces which he had at his dis-
posal—100,000 Mongols and others—would be enough to
subdue Persia and Afghanistan and to defeat Jelal ed-Din.

Sabutai then told Genghis about a plan that he and Jebei
had been discussing. They wanted approval to ride around the
Caspian Sea and to cross the Caucasus Mountains and see
more of the "people with narrow faces, light hair and blue eyes"
of the West. He suggested to Genghis that such a reconnaissance
might be useful for future Mongol campaigns. Genghis approved
the request, and Sabutai rode back to rejoin Jebei on the
Caspian.

Conquest of Khorassan

Genghis' youngest son, Tuli, was now sent into Khorassan to
continue the conquest which Sabutai and Jebei had begun in
their chase after Shah Mohammed. Tuli seriously set to work
in his first important independent operation, which was more
difficult than Genghis had expected. The cities that had sub-

77

mitted so quickly to Jebei and Sabutai had now decided to defend themselves. But Tuli's troops captured Merv on February 25, 1221, and Herat on April 10. Each city was reduced to ruins and the populations massacred, after the slaves, artisans, and healthy young men for the armies were selected.

Since the Moslem population of south and southwest Persia was beginning to unite behind Jelal ed-Din, Genghis had ordered his troops to revert to terror tactics. The 100,000 Mongols in a hostile, densely populated land were fighting for survival as much as were the Moslems. It was a savage war on both sides and cruelty was common. From the reports of this warfare, written by Moslems, tales of Mongol atrocities began to circulate throughout the world.

Nishapur held out against Tuli for only three days. The death of Toguchar was avenged by savage destruction and slaughter that lasted for two weeks. As the word of the Mongol terror spread, Tuli's task became easier. He moved steadily through Khorassan, carrying with him death and destruction, reducing proud cities to desert, and removing whole populations in response to his father's commands. By fall he had completely overrun the region. Then, he turned southeast to join Genghis, whose campaign in Afghanistan had now become intensive.

Genghis had set forth in the spring of 1221 to find Jelal ed-Din and to disperse his army. In particular, Genghis wished to offset Jelal ed-Din's efforts to start a Moslem "Holy War" against the Mongols. He could see that this was beginning to strengthen the opposition of many of the cities of the old Persian Empire.

Genghis stormed and took the city of Balkh, the capital of

Bactria, just south of the Amu-Darya, and on the border of Transoxiana. Then he proceeded to take Talgan. Next he headed into the mountains of Bactria for the summer of 1221 to give his forces a few months' respite from the heat. These mountains divided Bactria (northern Afghanistan) from central Afghanistan.

In the fall, the Mongols left the highlands intending to move into central Afghanistan. However, the advance was held up by the mountain fortress of Bamian, protecting one of the main passes. Here Genghis' grandson, Moatugan, the son of Jagatai, was killed. Genghis ordered that Bamian be obliterated and its people annihilated in retaliation for this loss of one of his favorite grandsons. The place was never rebuilt.

Thus the bitterness and savagery of this war continued. There had been nothing like it in earlier conflicts in Mongolia, Hsi-Hsia, or China, where the defeated populations had been generally well treated, particularly if they supported the Khakan.

It was about this time that Jagatai and Ogatai returned from Urgenj, and Tuli from Khorassan. Soon after this, Genghis received word that Jelal ed-Din was at Ghazni, about 90 miles away, and that his army of about 10,000 men had destroyed a Mongol reconnaissance detachment of 1,000 men.

Genghis sent Shigi Kutuku with 30,000 men to find out what he could of the army being raised by Jelal ed-Din. At Parvan, Shigi Kutuku was ambushed and defeated by Jelal ed-Din, who had now collected an army of more than 50,000 men. Shigi Kutuku and most of his men were killed. Genghis now marched rapidly to Ghazni, and then to Parvan, seeking revenge. But Jelal ed-Din, after torturing and massacring the captured Mongols, had fled toward India. Genghis pursued relentlessly.

On November 23, 1221, Genghis overtook Jelal ed-Din on the banks of the Indus as the Turkish prince was preparing to cross the river into India. The two armies were closely matched in size; each was between 50,000 and 60,000 strong. Jelal ed-Din took up a defensive position beside the river, his flanks protected by mountains and a bend of the river.

The Battle of the Indus

The Mongols formed a semicircle around the Turkish army and began to close in at daybreak on November 24. Genghis ordered his soldiers to try to take the Khwarizmian prince alive, but not to let him escape. Genghis knew that if their leader were killed or captured Moslem resistance in Persia would cease.

At first the Mongols were successful, but a violent Turkish counterattack, led by Jelal ed-Din, almost broke the center of the Mongol army. Genghis rallied his men and sent a touman over apparently impassable mountains against Jelal ed-Din's flank. Struck from two sides, the Turkish defense collapsed. Jelal ed-Din fought like a tiger, even when the Mongol circle closed in upon him. Finally, he and seven hundred of his men were isolated and hemmed in on a cliff overlooking the Indus. He leaped on a fresh horse, jumped 20 feet into the Indus and swam across on horseback with a sword in his hand and his shield on his back.

Genghis, who was observing the action, greatly admired the courage, fighting skill, and resolution displayed by the Khwarizmian prince. Despite his earlier orders, he would not let his men shoot at Jelal ed-Din or follow him across the river.

The prince's followers, however, including two of his sons, were all killed. This Battle of the Indus decided the fate of the Khwarizmian dynasty. Although the bravery of Jelal ed-Din became a legend throughout the Moslem world, the Mongols had no further serious opposition in their occupation of the former Khwarizmian and Persian empires. Jelal ed-Din went to Delhi where he married the daughter of the sultan of Delhi. He later returned to Afghanistan. After Genghis' death he invaded Persia, but was routed by Mongols there and fled to die in Asia Minor.

In the spring of 1222, Genghis sent a touman into India. This was merely a reconnaissance raid and not an attempt at conquest. The Mongol detachment took Multan and Lahore, where the soldiers did some looting. They then returned to Afghanistan because they could not stand the heat of the Punjab summer.

Consolidation of the Khwarizmian Conquest

Genghis spent this spring in consolidating his gains and destroying sporadic resistance which had again flared up in Afghanistan and Khorassan. Ogatai went to Ghazni, where he slaughtered the inhabitants and destroyed the town, except for the skilled craftsmen selected to be sent to Mongolia. In Khorassan, rebellious Herat was taken again on June 14, 1222. The population was exterminated, the Mongols returning to massacre the few remaining people who crept out of hiding when they left.

Merv had been rebuilt and the river dammed again when the population learned of the victory of Jelal ed-Din at Parvan. The people rebelled and routed the small Mongol garrison, killing the regent left by Genghis Khan to govern them. The Mongols soon returned; the city was mercilessly ravaged and destroyed, and its population was massacred. Balkh, in Afghanistan, was given similar treatment. After these examples the people of the region lost all heart for resistance and the rebellion collapsed.

In the fall of 1222 Genghis returned to Transoxiana. He visited Bukhara and Samarkand again, then made camp outside Samarkand for the winter of 1222–23.

In March, 1223, while hunting, Genghis fell from his horse directly in front of a wild boar. The boar, amazingly, did not charge the stunned Khan, but stood glaring at him for a few seconds, then fled. From then on, following the advice of the Chinese sage, Chang-Chun, Genghis hunted no more. As a result of this incident he began to think about his age, about death, and about how to assure the future of this vast empire which he had acquired by hard fighting and brilliant planning. He consulted frequently with his principal administrative assistant, the Chinese prince, Yeliu-Chutsai.

Genghis entrusted much of the administration of the empire to Yeliu-Chutsai, whom he trusted completely. The Chinese prince did an exceptionally fine job, and organized the conquered regions for permanent domains, rather than as temporarily occupied territories. He persuaded Genghis to build up Karakorum as a capital city. This would be the imperial center to which people could look for systematic rule. Genghis himself had the roads developed throughout the empire, mainly for the efficient operation of his messenger system. Stations for food and fresh horses for the messengers were established at intervals to assure the speed which was required to keep the Khan in touch with the various portions in his empire.

Genghis, however, was never a city dweller. He was little affected by his growing power and wealth. He still wore the same clothes, had the same ideas of loyalty and simple courage, and loved the nomad life of his youth; he felt sure this life was superior to soft city living. He adopted little of the protocol and intricate manners of the Persian or Chinese courts. He valued above all else the comradeship of his old friends among the army, and of his wife of an earlier conquest, Kulan, princess from the tribe of Merkits.

Genghis spent a pleasant winter in Transoxiana. He had no problems with the people there, as he had had with the cities of the south and west. He lingered there, refreshing himself, his men, and their horses. In the late spring of 1223, however, he headed north again, to the region of Tashkent, on the northern bank of the Syr-Darya. Here he expected to be joined by Sabutai and Jebei, and to hear from them about their ride into Europe. He also expected that his eldest son, Juji, would rejoin him there. He sent for the other Mongol leaders, since he wanted to plan his route home and he wanted to discuss measures to be taken against the Hsi-Hsia for their failure to participate in the Khwarizmian expedition.

In the spring and summer of 1223, Genghis stayed in the valley south of Tashkent, with Tuli beside him. They were joined by Jagatai and Ogatai, who had been hunting in the region of Bukhara for a while. Late in the year he again began to move north by short stages, to return to the Irytsh in the summer of 1224.

Genghis was annoyed that Juji had not joined him. He summoned him again and prepared for a war against his eldest son when the prince did not come. Soon after this, however, he learned that Juji had died, and the emperor deeply regretted his harsh thoughts against his son. He resumed the march to Mongolia, and by the spring of 1225, Genghis and his Mongol armies were back again in their original camping grounds on the banks of the Tula River.

Meanwhile, late in 1224, Sabutai had joined Genghis, with the survivors of the force who had left Samarkand to pursue Shah Mohammed more than four years earlier. Possibly half of the 30,000 men had perished, including Jebei, who had died during the return march. Genghis insisted upon a full report from his favorite orlok.

CHAPTER 7

Reconnaissance to Europe (1221–1224)

Across the Caucasus

When Sabutai returned to the Caspian Sea winter quarters after his visit with Genghis Khan, early in 1221, he and Jebei at once began preparations for their bold expedition. By mid-March they were ready. First they moved westward into north-west Persia and Azerbaijan. Late in March they took Haragha; Hamadan was captured a few weeks afterward. They sent several scouts ahead to explore the region north of the Caucasus Mountains, while they ranged over the region between the Caspian and Black seas.

The Mongols invaded Georgia in the fall of 1221. Sabutai, leading the advance, was met by Georgian cavalry, assembled in the open field. After a sharp fight, the Mongols feigned retreat and led the Georgians into Jebei's ambush, where the Georgian army was wiped out. The Mongols did not stay to pillage Georgia, and Queen Russudan claimed that her knights had chased the Mongols out. But there was no promised Georgian contingent for the Fifth Crusade because there were not enough of Georgia's knights remaining.

Jebei and Sabutai headed north for the heights of the Caucasus Mountains. They had such a difficult time crossing the snow-covered passes that they had to abandon all their war machines and baggage. When the rugged mountain passage was completed, the Mongols met hostile warriors blocking the routes through the foothills to the steppes farther north. These were nomads of the mountains and the steppes: Alans, Cherkesses, Khazars, Bulgars, and Turkish Kumans. The ancestors of these pagan horsemen had come from central Asia—many of them from Mongolia—centuries before. They had been in several of the many Asian tides that had swept westward into Europe since before the dawn of history.

Now these nomads feared that Jebei and Sabutai's Mongols were coming to dispute their control of the Caucasian and south Russian steppes. They had assembled a large force, perhaps 50,000 men, to meet the Mongols at the exits from the passes. Jebei and Sabutai, knowing that their troops were not in good condition for battle, tried to negotiate with the opposing hordes.

The Mongols succeeded in breaking the Kumans away from the other tribes by promising to let them share the spoils of their raids. They also claimed kinship with them, and the appearance of the two peoples was quite similar. Jebei and Sabutai then easily defeated the remaining tribes. Following this, however, they turned on the Kumans and defeated them also. They chased the surviving Kumans across the Caucasus to the northern shore of the Sea of Azov, where the fugitives sought the protection of the Byzantium colonies.

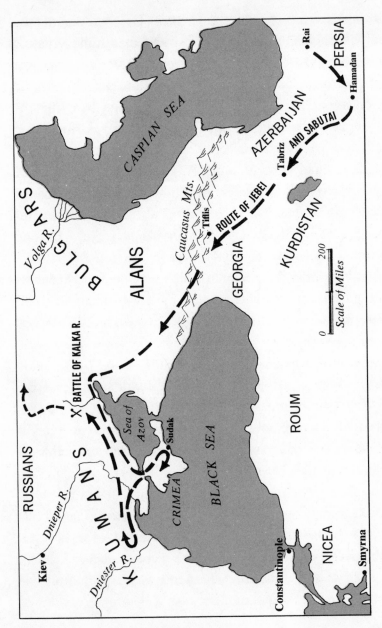

Route of Jebei and Subatai, 1221–1224

The Mongols went on into the Crimea. Here they had their first contact with western Europeans, when they took Sudak, a Genoese trading post. They then marched north and west across the Dnieper to the Dniester, where Jebei and Sabutai sought information about the peoples of eastern and central Europe: Russians, Poles, Silesians, Hungarians, Bohemians, and Germans.

One large Kuman tribe of south Russia had recently become allied with the Russian prince of Halicz (modern Galicia) through marriage. The Kumans had traditionally been Russian foes, but the prince was so worried by reports he had received about the Mongols that he gave his daughter to the Kuman khan in order to make an alliance. One wonders what the Russian prince thought of the bargain—and what his daughter thought—when he learned that the Kumans had been defeated.

The warring princes of Russia now realized that their region was threatened by a terrible foe. From the reports they received from the frightened Kumans, apparently they thought that Sabutai and Jebei had a host of more than 100,000 men. The Russian leaders agreed to forget their quarrels and formed a defensive alliance against the Mongols.

Early in 1223 Russian contingents from Novgorod, Moscow, Halicz, and other principalities met at Kiev. The Prince of Halicz then led this army of 80,000 men down the Dnieper toward the Black Sea, where the Mongols were camped.

Jebei and Sabutai, who had been spending a comfortable winter beside the Black Sea, and the Sea of Azor, were alarmed when they heard of the approach of this large army. Their mission was reconnaissance, not conquest. Jebei sent ten envoys to the Russians to seek peace. But the envoys were murdered by the Russians. So Jebei sent two more emissaries, volunteers, who faced death contemptuously to tell the Russians that they had provoked the Mongols into war.

Battle of the Kalka River

Jebei and Sabutai then marched north, probably with about 25,000 men, less than one-third of the Russian strength. The two armies met beside the river Kalka, on May 31, 1223. We do not know the details of the battle, but in a day of savage fighting the two brilliant Mongol generals destroyed the Russian army. Few of the Russian princes ever returned to the north.

There were no forces left in south Russia that could interfere with the Mongols. They rode unchallenged over the steppes, reaching the forests of central Russia before halting. They had no intention of invading Russia—yet.

Then, since the time allotted them by Genghis was running out, Jebei and Sabutai headed eastward toward Genghis' camp beside the Irtysh. On the way, they received the submission of the Bulgars on the Volga River. The Bulgars had heard what had happened to the Kumans and the Russians, and were terrorized before the Mongols reached their land.

Jebei died soon after this, while the little army was marching through western Siberia. Sabutai took command; a few weeks later he joined Genghis and gave a full report on the European reconnaissance. Sabutai proposed further conquest in the west. But Sabutai's knowledge of Europe had to be set aside for a later day when it could be turned to good use in a Mongol conquest. First, Genghis had on old score to settle with the King of Hsi-Hsia.

CHAPTER 8

The Last Campaign
(1225—1227)

Alliance of Hsi-Hsia and Chin

Genghis and his warriors had less than a year of rest in Mongolia after their return from the conquest of the Khwarizmian Empire. Affairs in Hsi-Hsia and in China soon forced the aging Khakan to take the field again.

The Chin and Hsi-Hsia empires had formed an alliance against Genghis. The new King of Hsi-Hsia had reportedly raised an army of 500,000 with which to defy the Mongols, while the Chin Empire was regaining strength after the death of Mukuli in 1223. Chin Emperor Hsuan-tsung also died that year and was succeeded by his son Shu-hsu. Under his more forceful leadership, Chin armies were striking north from Kaifeng fu, trying to recover lands north of the Yellow River which had been conquered earlier by the Mongols.

In the early spring of 1226, Genghis and a Mongol army of 180,000 warriors left Karakorum, prepared to deal with both the Hsi-Hsia and the Chin. Genghis was injured early in the march, probably during a border skirmish, suffering internal injuries from which he never recovered. He did not, however, stop the campaign, as many of his followers urged, but insisted that they go on. He did not wish the Hsi-Hsia to think the Mongols were weak. He continued on across the Gobi to northwestern Hsi-Hsia, confusing the Tanguts by taking a different route than in his earlier invasions.

The Mongols took Etzina, at the southern edge of the Gobi Desert, in March, 1226. That summer they took the cities of Kan-chou and Su-chou. In the fall, while Genghis rested in camp, his armies headed east; they took Liang-chou and moved on to capture Ying-li, 60 miles south of the capital, Chung-hsing, on the Yellow River. In December Genghis rejoined his troops and laid siege to Ling-chou, only 18 miles from Chung-hsing.

Battle of the Yellow River

The main Tangut army, possibly 300,000 strong, was sent out from Chung-hsing to relieve Ling-chou. Genghis retreated across the ice-covered Yellow River, enticing the Tanguts to follow. The iron horseshoes of the Tangut cavalry slipped on the smooth ice, slowing their pursuit. While the Tanguts were still crossing the frozen river, Genghis ordered a counterattack. The Mongols' shoeless horses could move much more securely on the ice, and they easily outmaneuvered the helpless Tanguts, slaughtering all of those on the frozen river. The main body of Tanguts, still on the opposite bank, were shaken by the disaster they were observing, when they were suddenly struck in a surprise attack from the flank by part of the Mongol army.

At the same time the main Mongol force continued its attack across the river. The Tanguts broke and fled, most of them slaughtered by the pursuing Mongols. Genghis then assaulted and captured Ling-chou, which was sacked. Genghis then permitted Yeliu-Chutsai to establish a new governmental administration in those parts of Hsi-Hsia which he had already overrun.

Genghis and his troops next moved on to the Hsi-Hsia capital, the large and bustling city of Chung-hsing. As the Mongols approached, the king fled to the mountains where shortly afterward he died or was murdered. Soon after his departure, in January of 1227, the invaders blockaded the city. The crown prince of Hsi-Hsia, who soon became King Li Hsien, had remained in Chung-hsing to command its defenses.

Genghis now decided that the outcome of the campaign was clear. His troops would soon capture Chung-hsing, and this would be the end of the Hsi-Hsia Empire. He left only about one-third of his army to complete the siege, while with the remainder he turned against the Chin. Ogatai, with half of this field force, was to strike due east into the heart of the Chin country. With the other half Genghis planned to march down the Yellow River.

The Last Days of Genghis Khan

In March, 1227, Genghis took Hsi-ning, on the caravan route to Tibet. In April he captured Lung-to. But his health was failing, and in late May or early June he set up a summer camp in the mountains of northwest China, where he lay very ill. Believing that he was dying, he sent for Ogatai and Tuli to come to him, so that he could give his two sons his final instructions for the immediate war, and also for the future of the empire.

When the princes arrived, Genghis painfully explained his campaign plans. Tuli was to obtain permission from the Sung to take part of the Mongol army through a corner of their domains in a bend of the Yellow River, to attack Kai-feng fu by a surprise advance from the southwest. Then Genghis gave instructions for the organization of the empire after his death.

Ogatai was to succeed as Khakan, the supreme ruler of the vast territories conquered by Genghis Khan. But each of his other sons, or his heirs, was to have lands of his own, under Ogatai. Juji's son, Batu, was to have all of the north and west, as far as land reached beyond the Altai Mountains. To Jagatai belonged the lands of the Uighurs, Kara-Khitai, and the Khwarizmian Empire. To Tuli he gave Mongolia and the Mongolian army—except his personal forces, which were to be divided among the sons and elder grandsons. Ogatai was to have all of the conquered lands of China and East Asia: the dominions of the Hsi-Hsia, of the Chin, and—eventually—of the Sung.

Genghis then ordered his sons and grandsons to act in unison and not to quarrel. In case of disagreement, all others must obey Ogatai, or his elected successor as Khakan. He told them about historical examples of what would happen if they did fall out, or if they failed to support each other in ruling the empire which he had acquired for them. All of this, he told them, was

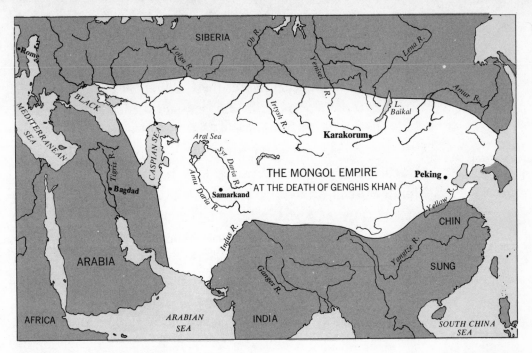

The Empire of Genghis Khan, 1227

spelled out in detail in his *Yasak*, the code of laws that was his will.

Genghis then gave two final orders. First, when Chung-hsing fell, the King of Hsi-Hsia was to be killed; all of his people were to be enslaved or killed. Secondly, his own coming death must be kept secret until the conquest of Hsi-Hsia was accomplished. Then Genghis Khan died, on August 18, 1227. He was sixty-five years old.

The Mongols vigorously pressed on with the siege of Chung-hsing. When King Li Hsien came out to surrender the city, they killed him, then assaulted and destroyed the city. Then Ogatai sent messengers into all the reaches of the Mongol lands informing the chiefs of the death of Genghis.

The body of the Khakan was then carried back to Mongolia in a funeral train. The sad trip was made in silence, out of respect to their ruler; in accordance with Mongol custom, the escort killed every person whom they met on the way. They took Genghis to the region where he had lived as a fugitive youth, Mount Burkan-Kaldun, where he was buried high on the mountainside. (In later years, his son Tuli, and Tuli's great sons, Mangu and Kublai, were also buried there.)

The manner of the funeral procession and last rites for Genghis were typical of the Mongol code—deep, sacrificing, and unlimited loyalty to their dead ruler, and utter contempt for all other peoples.

CHAPTER 9

Sabutai—the Continuing Spirit of Genghis Khan

Continued Mongol Expansion

Sabutai Bahadur, veteran orlok of many campaigns, and master of the art of war, continued to serve under Genghis' son and grandson with the same absolute loyalty which he had given to Genghis. In a very real sense, Sabutai was the continuing military spirit of Genghis Khan.

Genghis had chosen Ogatai to succeed him because, of his three sons still alive, Ogatai was the best judge of human nature, and the most reasonable. Yeliu-Chutsai, the able Chinese prime minister of Genghis, also favored Ogatai and sponsored his election to Khakan two years later when the kuriltai finally met to go through this formality. The administration of the empire went along very smoothly under Yeliu-Chutsai before Ogatai's election, and then until his death.

Meanwhile, under Tuli, the campaign against the Chin was carried to a successful conclusion in 1233 by the capture of Kai-feng fu, following the plan of Genghis. The principal strategist in this campaign was Sabutai, the man who best understood the system and the methods of Genghis Khan.

In 1235 Ogatai and the kuriltai decided to extend Mongol power still further by undertaking four simultaneous wars—in South China against the Sung dynasty; in Korea; in southwest Asia; and in Europe. It is amazing that the leaders of this small central Asian nation should have the audacity to plan to carry out even one of these ambitious operations, each several thousand miles from their homeland. It is incredible—and unmatched in history—that they should plan to do all four at once. Yet they were successful in all of them.

The Invasion of Europe

The conquest of Europe was considered the most important of these undertakings. The expedition was under the nominal leadership of Batu, Juji's son, because Juji had been given all the lands of the west. Sabutai, however, actually directed the European operation, and planned very carefully for this gigantic undertaking. He at once sent out spies to gain accurate information about European geography, and intelligence of all European rulers and national customs. He prepared an army of about 150,000 of the best Mongol warriors for a long series of campaigns. In his plans he allowed eighteen years for the subjugation of Europe.

Sabutai planned with foresight for European weather. In general, battles were to be fought, and traveling done, during the winter, when the ground would be solid enough for rapid movement and when frozen rivers could be easily crossed. Summers were to be spent in camp, refreshing the horses and men, drilling the army with its recruits from conquered lands, and planning the next campaign. The men would live off the land. They would take with them only what was really essential— the most important being many extra horses.

In the winter of 1236–37 the Mongols moved into the Volga country, where they easily subdued the Bulgars. Many Bulgars were recruited into the Mongol army, and trained extensively with the army during the summer.

In December, 1237, the Mongol expedition crossed the frozen Volga and went into completely new territory: central and northern Russia. The land which is now Russia was then divided into many principalities. It was a backward country; the people were hardly more culturally developed than were the Mongols.

Sabutai had decided not to ride across the steppes of southern Russia. This would give the Russian princes an opportunity to retreat, and to combine against him in the forests of the north. Instead he decided to enter Russia from the northeast. He drove his men in a rapid march first to the north, then west completely across Russia. They quickly took Ryazan, Moscow (then relatively unimportant), and Vladimir, the most important principality of the north.

By March, 1238, most of the northern Russian lands were in Mongol hands and the Russian armies utterly destroyed. There was no force to prevent the Mongols from sacking Novgorod, the leading city of old Russia. But Sabutai ignored Novgorod, since he wished to move south to the steppes before the snows melted. He knew the march would be terribly difficult in the mud of spring or the dust of summer.

The armies and horses rested from their travels in summer

camps in the area now known as the eastern Ukraine. But quarreling broke out among the Mongol princes. Kuyuk, Ogatai's oldest son, refused to fight under Batu or to accept his leadership. Eventually, at Sabutai's request, Kuyuk was recalled to Karakorum by Ogatai. It was probably because of this quarrel that the Mongols stayed for two years on the Ukrainian steppes. They were soon quite at home, and the Russians who inhabited the Don region came to be completely used to their presence. These unlimited grasslands, without fences or towns, were well suited to the Mongols' nomad existence. Later, when Batu became the first Khan of the Golden Horde, he established his capital city in similar surroundings farther east, at Sari on the Volga.

Into Central Europe

In November, 1240, Batu, Sabutai, and their army set forth again on what was to be one of the most momentous campaigns of history. The principal objective of the operations for the year was Hungary, then a well-established and rich kingdom under Béla IV. Here the Mongols apparently planned to make a permanent headquarters from which to conquer and administer the rest of Europe.

The campaign began with a whirlwind sweep across the Ukraine. They crossed the Dnieper on the ice and attacked Kiev, then the most important town in southern Russia, on December 6. Within twenty-four hours the Mongols had fought their way into the city. A few hours later Kiev was a smoking ruin.

The Europeans knew nothing of the Mongols, or their origin, or their methods of making war. But word of the sack of Kiev spread across eastern Europe, and suddenly it was apparent that a new and unknown force was threatening Christendom. The princes of eastern Europe began to call up their forces to meet the Mongols. Boleslaw, the King of Poland, organized his people, and Prince Henry the Pious of Silesia hastily assembled an army of 30,000—Silesians, Bavarians, Teutonic Knights, and Templars from France. King Wenceslaus of Bohemia raised a force of 50,000 Bohemians, Austrians, Saxons, and others. Meanwhile, in Hungary, King Béla began to assemble an army of about 100,000 Magyars, Croats, Germans, and French Templars in his capital city of Buda.

As the Mongols marched west from Kiev, Sabutai divided the army into three separate hordes. Prince Kaidu with two toumans—20,000 men—was to march northwest into Poland, then west and south through Bohemia to join the main body in Hungary. To the south, Prince Kadan was also to take two toumans through the southern Balkans and then turn north into Hungary. The main body of 80,000 men, under Batu and Sabutai, was to strike due west across the Carpathians into the plains of Hungary. Sabutai left about 30,000 men to hold the conquered regions in Russia.

Kaidu swept north into Poland on a broad front. One of his toumans reached the Baltic. With the other touman Kaidu met and defeated Boleslaw in central Poland on March

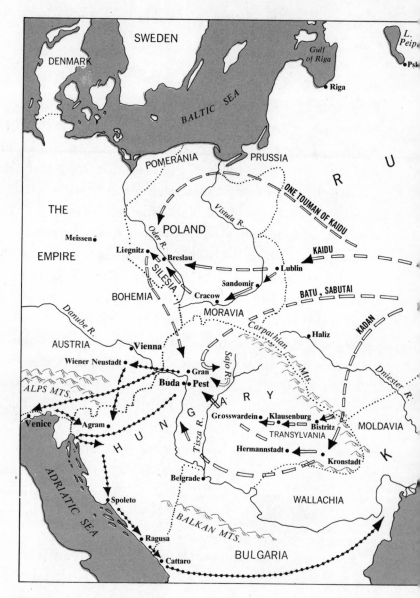

The Mongol Invasion of Europe, 1237–1242

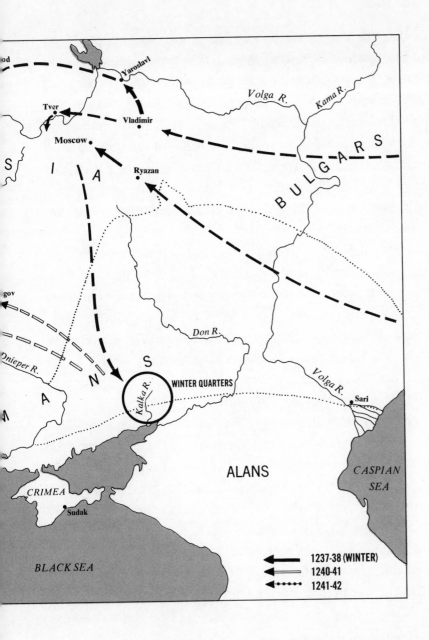

Yaroslavl

Volga R. *Kama R.*

Tver

Vladimir

Moscow

Ryazan

B U L G A R S

S   I   A

gov

Don R.

N

Dnieper R.

A   S

A   M

Kalka R. **WINTER QUARTERS**

Volga R. Sari

ALANS *CASPIAN SEA*

CRIMEA

Sudak

BLACK SEA

1237-38 (WINTER)
1240-41
1241-42

18, 1241. Then on March 24 he took and burned the famous old town of Cracow. About this time, Kaidu learned that Prince Henry of Silesia was planning to join forces with King Wenceslaus, and he decided to hit Henry before this meeting could take place. Near Liegnitz, on April 8, the other toumans rejoined Kaidy. Next day the Mongols caught up with Henry and smashed his army in a desperate battle. At least half of Henry's force of 30,000 men were killed, including Henry and most of his noblemen and knights. Mongol losses were also severe in the bitterly contested struggle.

After the battle, the Mongols paraded around the town of Liegnitz with Henry's head on a pike. This was part of their deliberate campaign of terror, designed to convince their enemies that they should give in without resistance. This psychological warfare, along with the unusual speed and mobility of the horsemen, gave them a reputation among Europeans for being completely inhuman, and also for being much more numerous than they actually were.

The next day, Kaidu began to march against King Wenceslaus who had a cumbersome European medieval army of 50,000 men about 50 miles to the south. But, despite their victory, at Liegnitz the Mongols had gained great respect for the effectiveness and stubbornness of European chivalry. So Kaidu decided to leave Wenceslaus alone, ravaging Silesia and Moravia instead. He then pretended to head west, but actually he turned south to join the other Mongol armies in Hungary.

To the far south the horsemen under Prince Kadan took Bistritz, Klausenburg, and Grosswardein as they moved across Transylvania. Two days after the Battle of Liegnitz they defeated a Magyar army outside the fortress of Hermannstadt, which they then assaulted and captured. After that Kadan marched north to meet Sabutai, Batu, and Kaidu in central Hungary.

Meanwhile Batu and Sabutai, with the central Mongol army, fought and won several minor engagements on the road to Pest. Despite this opposition, they moved from the snow-covered passes of the Carpathians some 200 miles in the four days between March 12 and March 15. They appeared outside Pest just as Béla was calling a council of war in Buda, across the Danube. He had received word that the Mongols had crossed the Carpathians and so was astonished to find them already at the gates of his capital.

While the Mongols devastated the countryside, Béla moved his army of 100,000 men across the river to Pest. Sabutai then pretended to retreat to the northeast, for about 100 miles. Béla and his army followed to the Mohi Plain, reaching the Sajó River on April 10. The Mongols pretended to continue their retreat, crossing the river and leaving Béla in command of the plain and of the only bridge across the river. He camped for the night beside the bridge, forming his wagons into a wall around his camp. He sent a small force to hold the far end of the bridge.

Battle of the Sajó River

Just before dawn next morning the Hungarian bridgehead defenders found themselves under a hail of stones and arrows, "to the accompaniment of a thunderous noise and flashes of fire." Some historians believe that the Mongols were actually using the first cannon of European military history. This is doubtful. More likely, it was their usual employment of catapults and ballistae, using Chinese firecrackers to increase terror. In any event, this was a thirteenth-century version of a modern artillery preparation. It was followed closely, as in modern tactics, by fierce assault.

The defenders of the bridge, stupefied by the noise, death, and destruction, were quickly overwhelmed and the Mongols streamed across. Béla's main army, aroused by the commotion, hastily sallied out of the fortified camp. A bitter battle ensued. Suddenly it became evident, however, that this was only a Mongol holding-attack.

The main effort was made by three toumans, some 30,000 men, under the personal command of Sabutai. In the predawn darkness he had led his troops through the cold waters of the Sajó River, south of the bridgehead, then turned northward to strike the Hungarians' right flank and rear. Unable to resist this devastating charge, the Europeans hastily fell back into their camp. By 7:00 A.M. the laager was completely surrounded by the Mongols. For several hours they bombarded it with stones, arrows, and burning naphtha.

It appeared to some desperate Hungarians that there was a gap in the Mongol lines to the west. A few men galloped out safely. As the intensity of the Mongol assault mounted elsewhere, more and more discouraged and frightened defenders slipped out. Soon a stream of men was pouring westward through the gap. As the defense collapsed, the survivors rushed to join those who had already escaped. Losing all semblance of military formation, many of the fugitives threw away weapons and armor in order to flee better.

Suddenly the escaping soldiers discovered that they had fallen into a Mongol trap. Mounted on swift, fresh horses, the Mongols appeared on all sides, cutting down the exhausted men, hunting them into marshes, and storming the villages in which some of them attempted to take refuge. In a few hours of horrible butchery the Hungarian army was completely destroyed, with between 40,000 and 70,000 dead.

Not more than 20,000 Europeans survived the battle and the pursuit. Béla managed to escape and fled west across Hungary. But he had neither the resources nor the will to fight the Mongols again. The Mongols pursued him across Croatia and Dalmatia, but he finally escaped to an island in the Adriatic.

The victory at the Sajó River assured Mongol control of all eastern Europe from the Dnieper to the Oder and from the Baltic Sea to the Danube. In four months they had overwhelmed Christian armies totaling five times their own strength.

The Threat to Western Europe

The Mongols settled down in Pest, and across eastern Hungary. Europeans writing in that era reported that Hungary had ceased to exist and had been completely taken over by the "Tartars." Apparently the Mongols planned to stay in Hungary, because they set up an occupation administration, called back the townspeople with promises of safety, and persuaded them to return to their tasks. Also, they had coins struck with Hungarian place-names on them.

On Christmas Day of 1241 the Mongol invasion of central Europe began, as Sabutai's soldiers streamed across the frozen Danube. They soon took Buda, Gran, and other western Hungarian towns. The advance guard pressed into Austria as far as Nieustadt, near Vienna. Mongol scouts raided across the plains of northeastern Italy past terrorized Venice. Had it not been for an unusual turn of events in the Mongol world itself, it is likely that all Europe would soon have shared the fate of Russia and Hungary.

But early in 1242 Batu and Sabutai received a message which had come 6,000 miles from Karakorum to Austria. Ogatai was dead.

Batu wanted to remain in Europe and continue the conquest. But Sabutai reminded him that the Law of the Yasak and the decree of Genghis Khan required all princes and chiefs to return to Karakorum for a kuriltai and the election of a new Khakan. The Mongol armies turned and marched eastward. As far as the Europeans were concerned, the Mongols had vanished as mysteriously as they had come.

The Mongol Empire After the Death of Genghis Khan

The Succession

Genghis Khan allocated his empire among his sons before he died, but he did not intend the Mongol Empire to be partitioned. Rather, each son was to obtain taxes and tribute from his immediate realm, and was to command the Mongol armies which might be fighting in his area of interest and responsibility. But the empire as a whole was to be subject to a Great Khan, successor of Genghis, who was to be chosen for his ability by a kuriltai of all the Mongol leaders. As we have seen, Ogatai was Genghis' choice for the first Khakan to follow him, subject to the approval of the kuriltai.

The domains of the sons of Genghis were distinguished by colors, since few Mongols could read or write. White was the color of the western lands, from the Irytsh north and west, as far as a horse could travel, which first belonged to Juji, and after his death, to his son Batu. Blue was the color of the east—the realm of the Chin, Hsi-Hsia, Manchuria and Korea, and the yet unconquered Sung Empire in the south of China

—the region given to Ogatai. Red was the color of the south and southwest: Kara-Khitai, the Uighur lands, and the Khwarizmian Empire, which went to Jagatai. Tuli, the youngest, was by Mongol tradition regarded as the keeper of the hearth; to him were assigned Mongolia and the Mongol army, distinguished by the colors of the rainbow.

For most of the thirteenth century things went as had been decreed and planned by Genghis. Each of the domains was enlarged after his death. There was a Khakan, as commanded by the Yasak, who was supreme, receiving homage and gifts from all the then-known world, a force to be reckoned with wherever men traded or fought. The four great Mongol Khakans after Genghis were: Ogatai (1229–41); Kuyuk, the son of Ogatai (1246–48); Mangu, the son of Tuli (1251–59); and Kublai, the third son of Tuli (1260–94).

But there was dissension among the princes from the beginning. Ogatai, then Mangu, and finally Kublai inherited enough of the greatness of Genghis to hold the empire together. But after the death of Kublai the empire soon disintegrated. Each of its four major regions went its separate way. These events are briefly traced below.

The East—Mongolia and China

Genghis had given Tuli a plan for defeating the Chin by an alliance with the Sung. This plan was carried out by Tuli from 1230 to his death in 1232 and then continued by Sabutai.

Kai-feng fu was taken in 1233. At the request of Yeliu-Chutsai, the city's population of 2,000,000 was spared. This encouraged the remaining Chin provinces to submit to the Mongols, and the last Chin emperor committed suicide. The Mongols were now supreme in all of northern and western China.

The Mongols coveted the Sung lands to the south, but the Sung had been their allies against the Chin. However, the Sung were secretly discontented with their allotment of the Chin lands after the war, and so mobilized to fight the Mongols. This gave Ogatai and the other Mongols the opportunity they wanted, without the dishonor of attacking an ally. But Ogatai died before war could be declared on the Sung. However, before his death, Ogatai had sent an army into Korea at the same time that Batu and Sabutai went off to conquer Europe.

After the death of Ogatai there was nearly a civil war among the jealous princes before Sabutai and Yeliu-Chutsai prevailed upon them to accept Kuyuk, who was proclaimed Khakan at a kuriltai in 1245. When Kuyuk died, in 1248, the quarrel broke out anew. The sons of Tuli (Mangu, Hulagu, Kublai, and Arik-Buka) joined with Batu, the son of Juji, to oppose the claims of the descendants of Ogatai and Jagatai. Mangu was selected as Khakan, and Kublai was made viceroy of China. To reunite the Mongols the kuriltai decreed that they should conquer the Sung and add south China to the Mongol Empire.

Kublai, Chinese-educated and a gifted leader, had been a favorite grandson of Genghis as a child. In 1252–54 he began the invasion of the Sung domain from Chung-hsing in Hsi-Hsia. He advanced through the mountains of Tibet with an army of

100,000 men, heading toward the southern Sung territories by way of the kingdom of Nan-Chao. With Kublai went Sabutai's son, orlok Uriangkatai, who took the city of Yunnan, in the Nan-Chao province of Yunnan, while Kublai took Tali. No Mongols or inhabitants were killed in the occupation of Tali, where Kublai had banners carried through the city reading, "On pain of death, do not kill." Yunnan became a base for the final attack on the Sung.

In 1258–59, Mangu himself took the field against the Sung dynasty. He and Kublai each led one of the three Mongol armies that swept through the Sung lands of south China and Annam with fire and sword. Kublai took Hanoi, where he replaced his dead with native soldiers, drilling them and teaching them to fight in Mongol fashion. During this campaign, Mangu contracted dysentery and died.

In accordance with the will of Genghis Khan, after the death of Mangu, Kublai brought the campaign to a close and accepted the peace overtures of the Sung. The Mongols marched back to Mongolia, and in 1260 Kublai was elected Khakan in a kuriltai at Dolon-nor. Kublai also adopted the titles of the Emperor of China, and in China was known as the Emperor She-tsu, Son of Heaven.

Some of the Mongols, including several of Kublai's cousins, were displeased with Kublai's Chinese attitude. A rival kuriltai was called and it selected Kublai's young brother Arik-Buka as Khakan. Kublai soon proved he was a true Mongol general. He marched to Karakorum where he defeated the rival Khakan, whom he then pardoned. Prince Kaidu, Ogatai's grandson, also took up opposition to Kublai's reign, but Kublai followed him to the Altai Mountains and also defeated him.

Meanwhile Kublai had renewed the war with the Sung. He was determined to unite all of China. Finally, after a long siege, his armies took Hang-chou, the capital of the Sung and then the finest city in the world. The last Sung emperor, a boy of nine, was taken into Kublai's court. Resistance continued at Kuang-chou (Canton), but finally that city was taken in 1279. For the first time in three centuries, the entire Middle Kingdom of ancient China was under one ruler. Kublai, now unchallenged emperor of all China, was the founder of the Yuan dynasty. He established his capital at Peking.

Kublai had not destroyed the towns or the people whom he conquered, since he had wanted to restore China to its ancient power and prosperity. He promoted agriculture, the arts and sciences, and trade. He built and maintained good roads throughout China and to all the Mongol dominions as far as Persia and Russia. His messengers used the system established by Genghis Khan, and were able to cover as much as 300 miles in a day by having fresh replacements and fresh horses ready at each of the stations which were about 25 miles apart along the roads. He maintained a disciplined army, mostly Chinese, but based on the system of his grandfather, and with a core of the best Mongol troops. He appointed only Mongols, Persians, Turks, or Tibetans to the top civilian and military posts. He would not trust the Chinese to govern their own lands; if absolutely necessary, as in the garrisons, he would station southern Chinese in north China and vice versa. But these posts were changed every two years to prevent graft, corruption, and insurrection.

Kublai ruled China wisely and well for thirty-four years. He was adopted by the Chinese as their own ruler, rather than as a conqueror. When he died in 1294, the Chinese agreed that "he truly loved his people." But Kublai had been enough of a Mongol to leave instructions that he was to be buried beside the grave of Genghis, rather than in Peking. He was the last real Khakan, imposing both control and unity on all of the Mongol Empire.

Kublai's successors, however, were more Chinese than Mongol, and lost all influence on the other Mongol lands across Asia. And soon they lost influence in China as well. The reigns of these later Yuan emperors were short and marked by intrigues and rivalries. They were separated from both their Mongolian army and their Chinese subjects, and cared very little about the administration of the country. Soon China was torn by dissension and unrest; bands of thieves ranged the country without interference from the weakening armies of the Yuan.

The last of the nine successors of Kublai was driven from China by a peasant Buddhist, Chu Yüan-chang, a leader of one of the robber bands. Under his leadership, the south revolted and drove out the Mongolian garrisons. Chu set up a government at Nanking and for five years consolidated the former Sung domain and gained the loyalty of the Chinese people. Chu—now known as Emperor Hung-Wu, founder of the Ming dynasty—adopted Mongol military methods. Then,

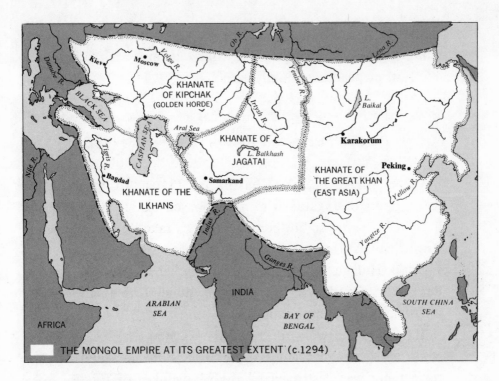

The Mongol Empire at its Greatest Extent, c. 1294

with an army of 250,000 he drove the Mongols out of north China and forced them back into the Gobi Desert. His army followed the Mongols into Manchuria and Mongolia and completely defeated them at the Battle of Puir Nor in 1388. Some 70,000 Mongols were made prisoner. The Chinese then captured Karakorum, which was destroyed.

The Mongols reverted to the tribal life and disunity they had known before Genghis. They continued border skirmishes with the Ming, however, and the Ming emperors renewed the ancient Chinese policy of dividing the tribes against each other until 1571, when peace was finally made.

The Southwest—the Ilkhans

When Mangu became Khakan in 1251, he dispossessed the descendants of Jagatai, who had opposed his election. In 1255 he sent his younger brother, Hulagu, to take charge of the old Khwarizmian Empire, which had been the inheritance of Jagatai. Hulagu extended and strengthened Mongol rule in Persia, Iraq, and Syria. He became, under Kublai, the first of the Ilkhans, rulers of the south.

When Hulagu went to attend the kuriltai in 1260, after the death of Mangu, his lands in Syria were invaded and his garrison there was destroyed by the Mamelukes of Egypt, under Sultan Baibars who had adopted the Mongol system of warfare. This was the first serious defeat the Mongols had suffered since Genghis Khan had become ruler of Mongolia. It also led to the first important war between grandsons of Genghis Khan. Baibars made an alliance with Bereke Khan, brother of Batu, and his successor as ruler of the Golden Horde. When Hulagu sent an army into Syria to punish Baibars, he was attacked by Bereke, and had to turn his army back to the Caucasus to meet this threat from his cousin. However, Bereke withdrew when Kublai sent 30,000 troops to aid Hulagu.

This chain of events marked the end of the Mongol expansion

in southwest Asia. The successors of Hulagu were unworthy descendants of Genghis Khan. They devoted themselves only to pleasure and let their provinces be governed by corrupt Turkish viceroys. Finally these viceroys seized control, and the Ilkhan Empire fell apart seventy-five years after it had been founded by Hulagu.

The West—the Golden Horde

The Golden Horde of Batu had more room for expansion of its territories than any of the other Mongol regions. Furthermore, the Golden Horde was not directly faced by a powerful enemy, or by an ancient civilization which could absorb it, and so this domain of Genghis' empire lasted the longest and had the most continued influence in the world.

The court of Batu at Sarai became a prosperous center of commerce under Bereke, who became a Moslem. Here, as in China, Mongol rule meant free trade and the transport of goods between the west and east and also the toleration of all religions. But the Mongols in the west remained a nomad people completely at home in the steppes of Russia. They preserved their simplicity along with their power, in part because they mixed with the Turkish tribes of the steppes to become the Tartars of Russia.

But the power of the Khan of the Golden Horde slowly declined, particularly as a powerful new state rose in central Russia. The princes of Moscow, vassals and tributaries to the

Mongols, took advantage of this weakness to assert independence under Ivan III in 1480.

One cause of the Mongol decline had been a bitter war against Tamerlane during the latter part of the fourteenth century. This Turkish conqueror claimed to be a descendant of Genghis Khan through the family of Jagatai, and he reunited all of Turkestan and the lands of the Ilkhans under his rule. In 1231 he invaded Russia, defeated the Khan of the Golden Horde, ravaged the Caucasus in 1395, and then withdrew.

The effects of this defeat, and internal struggles, led to the breakup of the Mongol, or Tartar, khanote in Russia into separate states. Three separate khanates—Astrakhan, Khazan, and the Crimea—lasted into the sixteenth century. The last reigning descendant of Genghis, Shanin Girai, Khan of Crimea, was deposed by the Russians in 1783.

The Mongols, or Tartars, through influence and intermarriage with Russian rulers, had a lasting effect in Russia. This Tartar heritage is part of Russia, making it distinctive from the nations of central and western Europe.

Military Career of Genghis Khan

1162	Birth of Temuchin.
1175	Death of Temuchin's father, Yesukai; Temuchin flees to exile.
1188	Temuchin defeats Targutai and becomes chieftain of the Kiut and Taijiut tribes.
1190	Temuchin chosen Khan of the Borjigin clan.
1194	Alliance with Togrul, khan of the Keraits.
1201–4	War against Jamuga, Togrul, and the Naimans.
1203	Temuchin defeats Togrul; becomes the leader of the Keraits.
1204	Battle of Chakirmont; Temuchin defeats the Naimans to become ruler of all Mongolia.
1205	First invasion of Hsi-Hsia.

1206	Temuchin is elected Khakan; takes the name Genghis Khan, and creates the Mongol nation.
1207, 1209–10	Invasions of Hsi-Hsia.
1209	Battle of the Irtysh River; conquest of the Kipchak tribes
1211–17	Invasion of the Chin Empire.
1211, April	Genghis crosses the Great Wall and begins campaigns in Shan-si and Chi-li.
1212	Second campaign against the Chin; support of Khitan revolt.
1213	Third campaign against the Chin; siege of Peking.
1214, April–May	Renewed siege of Peking; Chin sue for peace.
August	Chin renew war.
1215, May	Mukuli captures Peking for Genghis Khan.
1217, September	Genghis returns to Mongolia.
	Treaty with Shah Mohammed of the Khwarizmian Empire.
1218	Jebei's conquest of Kara-Khitai.
1219	Outbreak of war with Shah Mohammed; Mongol invasion of Khwarizmian Empire.

1220	Conquest of Transoxiana; flight of Shah Mohammed.
1221	Campaigns in Khorassan and Afghanistan.
1221, November 24	Battle of the Indus River.
1221–24	Expedition of Jebei and Sabutai to Russia.
1222–23	Consolidation of Khwarizmian Empire.
1223, May 31	Battle of the Kalka River, south Russia.
1225	Genghis returns to Mongolia.
1226, early spring	Genghis invades Hsi-Hsia.
December	Battle of the Yellow River.
1227, January	Siege of Chung-hsing begins.
August 18	Death of Genghis.
1229–41	Reign of Ogatai as Khakan.
1236	Mongols under Batu and Sabutai begin invasion of Europe.
1240, December 7	Capture of Kiev.
1241, April 9	Battle of Liegnitz.
April 11	Battle of the Sajó River.
	Death of Ogatai: Mongols withdraw from central Europe.
1246–48	Reign of Kuyuk as Khakan.
1251–59	Reign of Mangu as Khakan.
1260–94	Reign of Kublai as Khakan.

Appendix

Principles of Military Leadership and Military Theory

Since different people have different ideas about leadership, and about how it is defined and recognized, a few paragraphs are necessary to explain how the word "leadership" is applied in this book to the military career of one of the outstanding men of history.

Military Leadership

In its simplest terms, *leadership* means the ability of a person to influence and direct other people to work cooperatively together toward a goal or objective, because that individual commands their obedience, confidence, and respect. But these words are really meaningful only if we can relate them to observable standards of performance. One set of standards to show the qualities of a military leader is the following:

Professional military skill or competence. This includes a knowledge and understanding of past military events (or military history), an understanding of theoretical principles of warfare, and a combination of judgment and energy in applying this knowledge and theory to a variety of different situations.

Understanding of the human tools of the leader. This simply means that a leader must know the capabilities and limitations of his men.

Insistence upon high standards of training and discipline. In this way the leader, knowing his men, is able to make the most of their capabilities and to eliminate or reduce their weaknesses and limitations.

Inspirational ability. The leader must be able to project his personality to his men, so that they recognize the quality of his leadership and respond to it with confidence.

Personal courage. The leader must be able to set an example for his men. But in addition to willingness to face the dangers and risks of battle, he must have moral courage off the battle-field to make difficult decisions which lesser men might try to avoid.

Perseverance and determination in adversity. Some men can perform well when everything seems to be going their way. One important measure of human greatness is a person's ability to keep on striving for success, even when his best plans and actions seem to be resulting in failure.

The ability, in peace and war, to understand the relationship between military strategy and national policy. This is as true of a king-general, like Alexander the Great, or a civilian director of war, like Winston Churchill, as it is of the general who is controlled by civilian authority, like George Washington.

These are the seven standards, or yardsticks, of leadership which provide a basis for selecting the great captains. All of these standards are simple, and easy to understand, although their relationship together is so difficult that only a handful of men have been able to measure up close to the maximum of all of these standards.

The reader who is not intimately acquainted with military theory may find some problems with the first of the above standards, in recognizing the ability of a leader to apply military theory and principles to different situations. All that we really need to know, however, to understand the professional military qualities of military leadership which made the great captains great, is the nature of the principles of war and the relationship between strategy and tactics.

Military Theory

Over the past century, military theorists have formulated lists of *Principles of War* which are believed to include all of the fundamental elements of success in waging war. There are some differences among the lists prepared by different theorists, but since they are all based upon review and analysis of historical examples, these various lists are generally consistent with each other. There are differences of opinion as to the applicability of these principles to warfare in the future, but there is no doubt that they provide a useful measurement for past conflicts, since they are derived from, and based upon, the experience of the past.

In this series we use the following list of nine principles of war:

Objective. Every military operation should be directed to accomplish a decisive, realistic objective. The ultimate objective of any conflict is to destroy the enemy's capability and desire to continue the conflict. Intermediate objectives should contribute directly to attaining this ultimate objective. Objectives should be selected after due consideration of the characteristics of the area of conflict, and the resources and military forces which both sides can employ in the conflict.

Offensive. Only offensive action can achieve decisive results, since only by attacking or advancing can a military leader accomplish his objective by forcing his will on the enemy. Sometimes circumstances are such that a commander must take defensive action because the enemy is stronger, or in a more favorable position. But a leader on the defensive should always be seeking to find an opportunity where he can seize the initiative and press toward the achievement of his objective by offensive action. Other principles of war can help him in this search.

Simplicity. A commander must plan his operations and organize his forces so that they are as simple and uncomplicated as possible. When hundreds or thousands of men must work together to accomplish a plan, even the most simple plan may fail. The possibility for confusion and failure is even greater when men and commanders are frightened and excited in the course of a battle.

Control. (This is sometimes called "Unity of Command" or "Cooperation.") There must be one controlling authority to assure the decisive employment of all men and forces toward the achievement of an objective. This controlling authority achieves unity of effort by coordinating the actions of all forces available to him and assures cooperation between all of the individual people or forces engaged in the conflict.

Mass. (This is sometimes called "Concentration.") The maximum available combat power should be applied at the point and at the time which will best assure a decisive success. By seizing the initiative and concentrating forces rapidly and efficiently, a smaller force can often apply greater combat power at the decisive point than a larger enemy force. Mass is not dependent upon numbers alone but results from a combination of manpower, firepower, and fighting capability. Superior weapons, tactics, and morale can contribute to the effectiveness of mass.

Economy of Forces. (This is sometimes called "Economy of Effort.") A commander should employ only the absolute minimum of forces or resources at points which are not decisive. This will permit him to accomplish the principles of the objective and of mass at decisive times and places. Defensive action, or deception, at the less important points will help a commander achieve economy of forces.

Maneuver. Maneuver is the positioning, or the moving, of forces in such a way as to place the enemy at a relative disadvantage. By maneuver a commander can apply the principles of mass and the offensive at a decisive point where the enemy is not adequately prepared or positioned to meet an attack.

Surprise. This is accomplished by striking an enemy at a time, or in a place, or in a manner, that he does not expect. Surprise is particularly important for the commander of a force which does not otherwise have combat superiority to the enemy. Surprise can be achieved by speed, secrecy, deception, variations in fighting methods, and by moving through regions which the enemy does not think are passable for military forces.

Security. This means that a commander must take those measures which will prevent the enemy from surprising him, or from interfering with his operations. With adequate security, a commander can then apply the other principles of war, and employ his own forces in the most effective manner possible.

These principles of war are obviously very general in their nature; they apply to large forces and to small, and to extensive campaigns as well as to brief engagements. Military men usually say that they are applicable to both tactical and strategic operations. This means that the nonmilitary reader should have a clear understanding of the difference between strategy and tactics.

Many, many thousands of words have been written to describe strategy and tactics, and to explain the difference between the two terms. But really the distinction is not difficult.

Military strategy is the art of employing all of the resources available to a military commander for the purpose of achieving a successful outcome in a conflict against hostile armed forces.

Military tactics is the technique of assembling, positioning, and moving some specific portion of the forces available to a commander in order to contribute to the accomplishment of the goals or objectives of strategy.

In other words, strategy concerns the employment and disposition of all means of forces within a commander's power in order to achieve the desired result of a war or campaign. Tactics concerns the specific battlefield methods of employment of these means or forces.

Index